Dawn in Arctic Alaska

The University of Chicago Press, Chicago 60637
The University of Chicago Press, Ltd., London

Published 1957
University of Chicago Press edition 1985
Printed in the United States of America

94 93 92 91 90 89 88 87 86 85   5 4 3 2 1

*Reprinted by arrangement with the University of
Minnesota Press.*

Library of Congress Cataloging in Publication Data

Jenness, Diamond, 1886–1969.
  Dawn in Arctic Alaska.

  Reprint. Originally published: Minneapolis: University
of Minnesota Press, 1957.
  Includes index.
  1. Eskimos—Alaska. 2. Canadian Arctic Expedition
(1913–1918). 3. Jenness, Diamond, 1886–1969. I. Title.
E99.E7J5 1985   306'.08997   84–16153
ISBN 0–226–39741–6 (paper)

TO MY SONS

My Dear Boys:

I was still in my twenties when the events described in this book engulfed me, and, as happens so often, I doubted at the time whether they merited even the labor of a diary. Throughout the previous year I had been traveling among the natives of tropical New Guinea; and I had only recently returned from that region to my parents' home near Wellington, New Zealand when, early one morning, a breathless messenger-boy handed me a cablegram from Ottawa signed by a man named Sapir. As far as I now remember it ran as follows: "Will you join Stefansson Arctic Expedition and study Eskimos for three years? Reply collect."

I read and re-read this cablegram, bewildered. Ottawa, I knew, was the capital of Canada, and Sapir an official, presumably, of the Canadian government. But who was this man Stefansson who was to lead an expedition into the legendary Arctic? Would it not be well to know something about him before committing myself to an answer? Perhaps the Library of Parliament in Wellington could provide some information.

It did, and about a month later I found myself heading for Canada's westernmost city, Victoria. When I landed at that port, outwardly calm but inwardly still bewildered, a clerk at the principal post office handed me the following letter:

3

Ottawa, March 6, 1913

Mr. D. Jenness,
General Delivery,
Victoria, B.C.
DEAR SIR,—

I presume that the terms of your engagement have been made sufficiently clear in the cablegrams that you have received in New Zealand. Should there, however, be any doubt as to these in your mind, it may be well to briefly recapitulate. You are to spend three years in the Arctic regions of Canada as anthropologist on the Stefansson expedition, which is expected to leave Esquimalt, B.C. (not far from Victoria) late in the spring or early in the summer of this year. In consideration for your services you are to have all of your expenses paid for you from the time you have left New Zealand up to the time that you will have finished your field work. Moreover, during the three years among the Eskimo, you are to receive remuneration at the rate of $500 per year. This sum represents payment over and above all field expenses. At the end of the period of field work you are to work up your results for publication by the Anthropological Division of the Geological Survey of Canada. During this time, the duration of which cannot well be foreseen, you are to be under salary as one of the temporary staff of the Division of Anthropology. I may mention incidentally that your salary when working up results, as well as the $500 per year of field work, are to be paid out of regular Geological Survey funds, while the expenses of your trip are to come out of the appropriation set aside by the Dominion government for the Stefansson expedition.

In regard to the nature of your work, you will receive more explicit instructions from Mr. V. Stefansson, who is well acquainted with the general region and the character of the work to be done there. The main part of your work is to be the collection of a full ethnographical material, based on study and observation among the Eskimos of the Arctic region. In connection with your research work, it would be advisable for you to assemble rather full ethnographical collections from the various tribes visited, these collections to be forwarded to the Victoria Memorial Museum at Ottawa. As complete data should also be obtained on the physical characteristics of the natives visited, including systematic anthropometric data. To aid you in this work, we are sending you, under another cover, a set of anthropometric schedules. We are also sending you a set of face cuts which you will probably find useful in obtaining data on face painting, tattooing, and related subjects. Inasmuch as the technology of the

Eskimo has been more fully studied than any other phase of their culture, it is suggested that you concentrate as much as possible on the non-material side of culture, including such topics as religion, shamanism, social organization, and various beliefs and customs.

In conclusion, I may say that we are very glad indeed to have been able to procure your services for the expedition, and we hope that the interest of the work and the comradeship of the scientific staff will prove a source of pleasure to yourself. As already indicated, more specific instructions referring to the scene of operations and further details are to be obtained from Mr. Stefansson himself. If there is anything that we can do for you in the way of equipment or supplying further information before you set sail, or at any time thereafter, we shall be most happy to serve you.

Yours very respectfully,

E. SAPIR

From April 1 onward the members of the expedition began to gather in Victoria, but it was not until June 13 that Captain "Bob" Bartlett untied from the dock at Esquimalt our 250-ton flagship, the old whaling steamer *Karluk*, and slowly steamed her northward up the "Inside Passage" to the Gulf of Alaska, then west through Unimak Pass to the Bering Sea and Nome. On board the vessel were twelve scientists, the expedition's full staff apart from Stefansson, who lingered behind in Victoria to finish up some business and, traveling by the regular passenger steamer, joined us later in Nome. There he purchased two sixty-foot schooners, the *Alaska* and the *Mary Sachs*, to supplement the *Karluk*; and he divided the expedition into two parties, a northern and a southern, the former to travel on the *Karluk* under his direct command, the latter on the two smaller vessels. I belonged strictly to the southern party, which was to winter in the Eskimo territory around Coronation Gulf; but he attached me temporarily to the northern party because there was more passenger space on the *Karluk*. The three vessels were to rendezvous again near the mouth of the Mackenzie River.

Actually that season none of the three vessels ever did reach Herschel, the island near the mouth of the Mackenzie River that

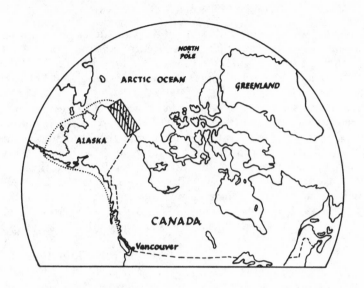

had been chosen as our rendezvous; for in this section of the American Arctic the laws of chance had decreed that once in every ten or fifteen summers a long, unbroken succession of westerly or northwesterly winds should press the polar pack ice tightly against the coast, rendering navigation difficult if not impossible; and we had happened on one of those summers. The ice wrecked not only our plans, but those of four other vessels that rounded Point Barrow, the most northerly point of Alaska, about the same time we did. They too had expected to go eastward, fulfill their various missions, then round Point Barrow again and return south before the summer season ended; but the ice both obstructed their missions and barred their return. At the time, we who were on the *Karluk* did not know the fate of our two schooners, the *Alaska* and the *Mary Sachs*. Later we learned that, being of shallower draft than the *Karluk,* they had navigated closer to shore inside a protective screen of islands and sand bars; and when the pack ice finally blocked all further progress they had found shelter for the winter in the safe harbor of Camden Bay. We on the *Karluk* were less fortunate. Early in August the ice hemmed us in ten miles northeast of Flaxman Island, only halfway, roughly, between Point Barrow and the Mackenzie

River. There we lay helpless, unable to move either forward or back even under full steam. Once, when we drifted quite close to Flaxman Island, Stefansson sent me out with another scientist to try to reach the shore; but the ice was too weak to bear the weight of our sleds and we had to turn back.

For a whole month the ice drifted slowly westward, holding our ship immovable in its grip; then the floes that surrounded us struck bottom in ten fathoms and remained fast. A week passed and still we did not move. Each day the weather grew a little colder and the ice more solid, until it seemed quite certain that the *Karluk* would remain there all winter. South of us, only fifteen miles away, was the delta of the Colville River where Stefansson had hunted caribou four years before. Why not hunt there again, and procure the fresh meat that would be so welcome after weeks of canned food? Stefansson decided that he would, and set about organizing a party.

He selected for companions, first, two Eskimos whom we had taken aboard before reaching Point Barrow. Neither of them was familiar with this part of the country, but they had hunted and trapped from boyhood and should know how to find their way about. Wilkins, our photographer, was the next most obvious choice, for although he was new to the Arctic (as indeed were we all except Stefansson himself and Captain Bartlett), he was one of those near-geniuses who can turn their hands successfully to anything. After Wilkins, Stefansson picked his secretary McConnell, a husky young man who had shown himself energetic and capable. Finally, at Wilkins' suggestion, he asked me if I would like to go with them, for I would at least gain some useful experience in sled traveling.

We left the ship about 1:30 P.M. on September 20, with two sleds each drawn by six dogs. That first day we traveled only five miles before setting up our tents, for the sea ice was rough and broken in several places and we were not fully familiar with our equipment. On the sleds we carried food for twelve days, although we anticipated being absent not more than seven. The second morning we started early, and in the middle of the afternoon

7

landed on the westernmost island of the Jones or Thetis group, a low deltaic sand bar lightly covered with snow and strewn with a considerable quantity of driftwood; from the top of an ice hummock stranded on its shore we could distinguish through binoculars the black masts of the *Karluk* some twelve miles to the north. On this island we spent the night and the next morning tried to reach the mainland three miles away; but the ice, which even on the previous day had been so thin that in patches it bent under the weight of our sleds, now became really dangerous, and we had to veer away to another island four miles farther east. From here open water was visible in two or three places, indicating that it would not be possible to cross to the mainland for perhaps a week. Stefansson therefore decided to wait where we were and, after we had eaten supper, wrote a note to Captain Bartlett which McConnell and one of the Eskimos were to carry back to the ship the next day. Meanwhile, the wind, which had been easterly all day, had increased a little, and the temperature seemed to be falling steadily.

When we awoke the next morning a blizzard was raging, and close to our island the ice had moved, opening up a few small lanes of dark water. Northward, between us and the now invisible *Karluk*, was a still wider lane, and there the ice seemed to be drifting westward. It was clearly unsafe for McConnell or anyone else to move off the island. All we could do was to wait.

We waited for six days, constantly scanning the horizon north of us. On the third morning Stefansson observed amid the white ice a dark spot which he thought might be the *Karluk* under full sail; and we hastily built a log platform to use as a watchtower. But the dark spot, whatever it was, moved steadily eastward and disappeared in the middle of the afternoon. Three days later we were able to cross to the mainland; but we never saw the *Karluk* again.

What happened to her you can read in Captain Bartlett's work *The Last Voyage of the Karluk*, which you will find on the top shelf of my bookcase. There you will find also Stefansson's monumental book *The Friendly Arctic*, which gives in an appendix another version of her fate. This book, based largely on Stefansson's personal diary, relates the history of our expedition from its inception in 1913 until his return from the Arctic in 1919. It does not tell the whole story, much of which lies buried in the diaries of other men. In front of me as I write, indeed, is the initial volume of my own diary, recording many scenes and events that have no place in Stefansson's history. It mirrors the northern coast line of Alaska, which changed greatly during the second quarter of the twentieth century and now reverberates with the noise of aeroplanes, tractors, and well-drilling equipment. Since my own experiences there preceded these changes, and differed greatly from the experiences of the other members of our expedition, I thought you might like to know something of what I saw and did during that first winter in the Arctic.

Your father,
DIAMOND JENNESS

THE *KARLUK* had disappeared. Whether the vessel had freed itself from the ice and steamed eastward, or whether, still imprisoned, it had been carried by the ice westward, we could not know. In any case it was gone, leaving our hunting party of six men marooned on a sandy islet surrounded by thin ice and open water. The wind finally died away, in the calm air the water rapidly froze over again, and on September 30 we crossed with our two sleds to the mainland.

For four days Stefansson and the two Eskimos scoured the countryside without finding a single caribou or other animal. We had shot a large seal and a dozen eider and old-squaw ducks while we were stranded on the islet; but these had provided hardly more than six meals for ourselves and our twelve dogs, and our food supply was beginning to run low. Where were we to go? There were no signs of habitation in the vicinity, no one to ask about the *Karluk* or to tell us whether our other two vessels, the *Alaska* and the *Mary Sachs*, had found shelter along the coast or perhaps reached Herschel Island, the first permanent settlement east of us and at least 300 miles away. Only 150 miles to the west, however, was the village of Barrow, and either there, or from Eskimos in its neighborhood, Stefansson thought we might gain some news of them.

We headed, therefore, for Barrow. The dogs, though on short rations, moved steadily forward over the smooth ice offshore at the rate of about three miles an hour. We knew from our chart that high mountains lay south of us behind the narrow coastal plain, but the haze that always blankets the land in early winter hid them from view. So low and featureless was the shore that from a short distance out it was impossible to tell where the sea ended and the land began. Every now and then we sighted a seal basking on the surface of the ice near a crack or breathing hole, and we halted while Stefansson or one of the Eskimos went off to stalk it; but there was so little cover that the animal invariably took alarm and dived out of sight before the hunter could approach within gunshot.

Two days passed uneventfully. Each morning we struck our tents at the first glimmer of dawn and pressed on, with only one short halt for lunch, until darkness began to close in around us about four o'clock in the afternoon. On the third day, near noon, we passed two sand bars known as the "Point Hope Islands" because many years before a war party of Point Hope natives had perished from starvation there after the local Eskimos had stolen their boats. Then, a mile or two farther on, we sighted a tent and a wooden platform on the shore line. Here, surely, were people. Veering south, we pointed our sleds in their direction.

A middle-aged man, tall and rather dark, came out to meet us. Although his features marked him as an Eskimo, the clothes he wore hardly differed from our own. He glanced rapidly from one to another, finally fixing his gaze on Stefansson, who, after a moment's hesitation, greeted him as an old acquaintance. His name, we learned, was Arksiatark, and his home lay inland in the basin of the Colville River, which he had descended only a month before in order to trap white foxes on the coast during the midwinter season, when the furs of those animals reach their prime. He told us that he had mistaken our party for that of his eldest son, who had sailed westward in the family skin-boat shortly before the freeze-up in order to purchase some supplies at Bar-

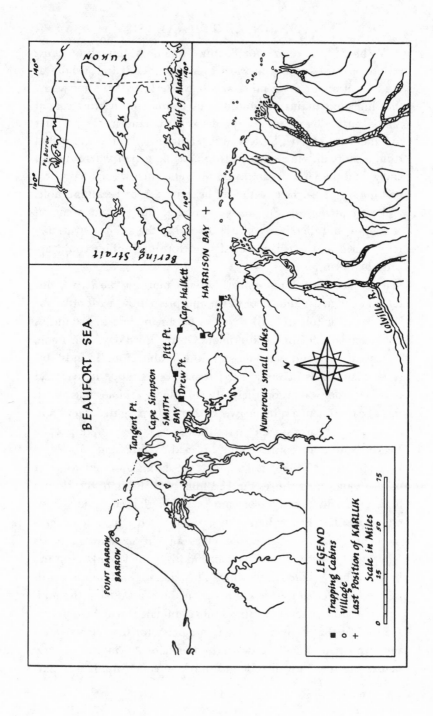

BEAUFORT SEA

POINT BARROW
BARROW

Tangent Pt.

Cape Simpson
SMITH
BAY
Drew Pt.
Pitt Pt.
Cape Halkett

HARRISON BAY +

Numerous small lakes

Colville R.

N

LEGEND

Trapping Cabins   ■
Village   ○
Last Position of KARLUK +

Scale in Miles

0   25   50   75

YUKON

ALASKA

Gulf of Alaska

Pt.Barrow

Bering Strait

row, but would doubtless return by sled now that the ice had closed in and rendered his boat useless.

Despite his evident disappointment, Arksiatark suggested that we pass the night with him; and he helped us to unload the sleds and pitch camp. His wife then came forward to greet us, and to invite us to partake of a meal in their tent, which was a patchwork of cloth stretched over an oval dome formed from willow twigs. We followed her inside, crawling one by one under the canvas flap that served as a door, and found ourselves in a space 9 feet long by 7 feet wide, but only 5 feet high. The flooring consisted of rough boards hewn out of driftwood; a rectangular stove fashioned from kerosene tins stood to the right of the door; and, scattered at the back of the tent, were bed skins of caribou fur and a few miscellanies. Evidently most of the family possessions had been stored outside on the wooden platform, which rose on four posts high above the reach of marauding dogs.

Like a party of school children, we sat in a row facing the stove and the doorway, changed our damp caribou-fur footwear, and handed it to our hostess, who deftly turned each article inside out and laid it over a cord or a stick just below the ceiling. She then blew up the fire in the stove, not pursing her lips as Europeans do, but curling her tongue into a kind of trough. While she was preparing the meal her husband invited us to wash, offering each of us in turn a small bowl of warm water, a fragment of soap, and a decidedly dirty towel. Wilkins, McConnell, and I, following Stefansson's example, politely declined; but our two Eskimos solemnly washed their faces and hands, neither daring nor indeed wishing to neglect this ritual that had recently spread along the coast.

Our hostess then laid before us an elaborate three-course meal: whitefish, uncooked but frozen, with a cube of raw caribou fat as an appetizer and a dish of rancid seal oil for seasoning; boiled ptarmigan; and whitefish that she had boiled whole, without removing either heads or tails. To complete this lavish repast she served us hot tea, for which we produced our own cups. Although there were several pans and kettles inside the tent, and flour,

to store away only four caribou carcasses, and his partner (for Eskimos seldom hunt alone) only six, although they had scoured the greater part of the Colville River basin. Seals were plentiful enough along the coast, but the sea ice was still much too thin to harpoon them at their breathing holes; in any case he himself had never practiced that craft of his coastal kindred. Instead, he and two other families had set seines under the ice of a lake some fifteen miles from the camp in which we now found him, and there each day they were pulling in scores of whitefish, which froze to solid stone almost as soon as they were thrown out onto the surface of the ice.

Stefansson accompanied him to the lake the next morning, since we sorely needed food for our hungry dogs; and the two men returned after dark with a load of 258 fish, each weighing on the average about three pounds. They brought with them also the middle-aged wife of another fisherman named Kunarluark, whose son had gone to Barrow with Arksiatark's son. Neither Mrs. Kunarluark nor her husband spoke any language but Eskimo, yet one of their daughters had married a white trapper, Ned Erie, who was living about two hundred miles to the east near Barter Island, and the other a Japanese who owned a hotel somewhere on the Yukon River. The courtships could scarcely have been garrulous, since the two bridegrooms knew only a few words of Eskimo; but speech differences have never proved an insuperable barrier to mixed unions, even in civilized lands, and in such frontier regions as Arctic Alaska they form hardly any barrier at all.

Heading northwestward from Arksiatark's camp we struck after seventeen miles the neck of Cape Halkett and began to cross its two lagoons to the sea on the opposite side. Here Wilkins expertly speared a young white fox which our dogs had routed out of its burrow in a cutbank, but the thin, yellowish pelt was practically valueless, being not yet in its prime. Six miles beyond the cape we saw smoke issuing from two log cabins, an indication that the Barrow Eskimos had already begun to spread east and south along the coast in preparation for the winter's trapping, and were now settling down, generally two families together, at intervals of ten to fifteen miles. As we halted in front of the cabins their occupants tumbled briskly out of the doorways and shook our hands with a friendly "hallo," after which the women disappeared indoors again while the men helped us to unlash our sleds.

This mode of greeting, half-European, half-native, we were to experience again and again, for it had become quite standardized throughout Arctic Alaska. A visitor seldom received a formal invitation to remain, but entered unasked whatever cabin he chose, taking with him his bedroll and, if possible, some sugar, butter, tea, or other contribution to help out his hostess' stock. In the corridor outside the door he paused a moment to beat the snow from his caribou-fur clothing, which would shed its hair if it became damp and lose nearly all its insulating properties. Entering, he sat on the floor facing the doorway and removed his mittens, his boots, and, if necessary, his parka, which he handed one after the other to his hostess to hang up for drying somewhere near the stove. He then relaxed and exchanged the latest news with the inmates while she stirred up the fire and mixed some dough. Half an hour later visitor and hosts would be squatting around a basin of hot biscuits in the middle of the floor, each person armed with a cup for the inevitable tea. Fish or meat supplemented the biscuits if it was evening, when the Eskimos ate their principal, sometimes indeed their only meal. Little children dined apart from their elders; and, if the room was crowded, one or more of the women waited at the back of the dwelling until the men had finished and moved back. After all were satisfied the hostess tidied up the floor and performed her last duty toward her guest: she carefully examined his boots and mittens to make sure that they were dry, mended any rents that she discovered, and sewed on any necessary patches.

Such was the standardized welcome the traveler received when he arrived at an Eskimo's cabin. Standardized in this region, too, were the cabins themselves, for they were all built of the same materials, and on very much the same plan. Of course, some were larger than others, and their interiors possessed conveniences such as sleeping benches that others lacked. There were cabins with one room only, and cabins with two rooms side by side, or one behind the other. These variations, however, were insignificant. What one may call the standard cabin was a rectangular dwelling about 10 feet long by 12 feet wide, with a gabled roof 5 feet high at the front and back and 7 feet in the middle, where alone it was possible for a man to stand upright. It had walls of untrimmed driftwood logs set perpendicularly side by side, and a roof and flooring of similar logs flattened on one face. The door, 4 feet high and hinged with leather straps, faced southward, and the roof above it contained a skylight that was "glazed" with a seal intestine slightly domed to catch more light. This intestine possessed the opaqueness of celluloid, and, though very thin, was strong enough for the housewife to scrape off the frost and to stitch up any rents.

A layer of turf encased both roof and walls, and, with its mantle of snow, rendered the dwelling virtually air-proof. Indeed, if the door had fitted at all closely, the inmates would have suffocated whenever they lit their stove, for the temperature at such times often exceeded 100°F.; but the door hung very loosely, as a rule, and the covered passage that led up to it, 15 feet or more long, about 3 feet wide, and 5 feet high, formed a natural channel for an inflowing draft. The passage itself was built from snow blocks supported by a framework of timber; for these Alaskan Eskimos, unlike the Eskimos farther east, did not know how to make a domed roof from snow blocks alone. Its entrance was sometimes closed by a cloth or skin to keep out the drifting snow; more often, it was left wide open, but pointed away from the prevailing wind. In summer the dwelling rose prominently above the bare ground; but in winter the snow that drifted over it reduced it to a low, almost imperceptible mound where only the dark, gaping hole of its passage entrance, and the tip of the black stovepipe protruding above the white snow, betrayed the presence of a human habitation in the otherwise featureless landscape.

The inside of each cabin matched the primitiveness of its exterior. The walls were quite bare, with turf visible between the logs in many places. Caribou skins and sleeping bags littered more than half the floor, and two or three boxes containing tools and miscellaneous trifles generally lay secreted somewhere against the back wall. A log stretching right across the floor from one side wall to the other separated the back "bed-and-parlor" section of the room from the "kitchen," which held nothing but a stove to the right (or left) of the door, a light crib of sticks above the stove for drying damp footwear and mittens, and, in the corner, a few utensils for cooking and eating. When the sun was shining — from mid-November until mid-February the sun never rose above the horizon — the intestine window above the stove transmitted just enough light for the housewife to cook and sew; but the more prosperous families always possessed at least one kerosene-burning hurricane lantern, while many others used homemade contraptions that burned seal oil or whale oil. Most of the household possessions were not brought inside at all, but were cached out of doors on a high wooden platform. It was there that the families kept their stores of food, their bags of spare clothing, their weapons, sleds, and dog harnesses. It mattered little that these objects should be fully exposed to the weather, or lie buried all winter beneath a mound of snow. What did matter was that they should be out of reach of the ravenous sled dogs, which habitually slept beneath the platform except when severe blizzards or extreme cold drove them for shelter into the passageway.

Of the two cabins we had now stumbled upon near Cape Halkett one conformed exactly to the above description; but the occupants of the other had slightly modified the usual plan by expanding the front part of the house sideways, thus giving it the form of a Latin cross. A chill draft that blew through the chinks in its walls made the interior rather uncomfortable; but the winter was still young, and the dwelling promised to be very snug later in the season after the snow had drifted over it. I saw among its furniture a hand sewing machine and a primus stove, articles that had been current in the region for perhaps a quarter of a century. The primus stove, indeed, had become a real necessity, because now that these Eskimos had taken to trapping foxes in winter instead of hunting seals on the sea ice, they had abandoned their old cooking lamps that burned seal blubber and adopted in their place wood-burning stoves of the European type, which they could easily fashion from empty kerosene tins. From Barrow eastward, however, there was no wood away from the coast, since the country was treeless; and even on the coast wood could no longer be found in every locality. It came from one source only, the Mackenzie River, several of whose tributaries tap the great forests in the eastern foothills of the Rocky Mountains. From the delta of that river the winds and currents had carried the floating logs westward and strewn them along the shore, in some places very thickly; but these large accumulations were the product of many centuries, and there were places, especially near Barrow, where the excessive inroads of the Eskimos had already exhausted, or nearly exhausted, the slowly gathered piles. Hence at this period no one ventured to travel without a primus stove and kerosene, except during the summer months.

Having on hand two cabins that were willing to receive us, we left our tents on the sleds, and three of us carried our sleeping bags into one cabin while the remaining three made their way into the other. However, we all gathered in the larger one for dinner, when our hosts set before us, in addition to biscuits and tea, slabs of cold boiled meat from an inquisitive polar bear that one of them had shot near the camp the previous day. They then plied us with questions, asking us where we came from and why we were heading for Barrow; but of the *Karluk* they could tell us nothing, having neither seen nor heard of any vessel imprisoned in the ice pack off their coast.

We left them at daybreak, harnessing up our dogs and driving away without a word of acknowledgment or farewell. Some of our hosts had already gone hunting, the others remained indoors and did not trouble to come outside even to witness our departure. It was not that we or they showed any breach of courtesy. Eskimos welcome the coming guest, but never speed the departing.

That day we traveled about twenty miles, stopping finally at three empty cabins that stood on the seashore forlornly awaiting their owners. The next morning we started early, hoping to reach Barrow in two days; but, veering unconsciously westward, as one is apt to do in foggy weather, we found ourselves most unexpectedly near the bottom of Smith Bay. A right-angle turn brought us out of the bay to Cape Simpson; but by that time darkness had set in, forcing us to halt and pitch camp. As we sat talking after the evening meal one of our natives casually told us that there was a strange lake of "pitch" a few miles inland which poisoned any bird or animal that drank from it; he himself had found an owl lying dead on its shore. I entered his remark in my notebook and promptly dropped it from memory; but twenty years later rumors of this lake that reached the outside world instigated a vigorous oil rush, which collapsed only when the United States navy stepped in and proclaimed the whole region a government oil reserve.

From Cape Simpson we were able to follow some well-marked sled trails that ran between the mainland and a line of sand bars a mile or so offshore. The ice had piled up in great ridges on the outer side of the bars, but on their inner side it was as smooth as a billiard table, although so thin that every now and again it bent alarmingly under the weight of our sleds. We observed several fox tracks, and also the footprints of a polar bear. Bears were evidently not uncommon in this area: three had already been shot by the few Eskimos we had met since leaving the ship.

Toward noon we came upon a settlement of two cabins, with whose occupants we stopped to eat lunch. There were six of them, a man named Angopcana, a boy, and four women. Angopcana was afflicted with a slight impediment in his speech; and of the women one was totally blind, another paralyzed in the right leg and right arm, and a third so old that she could remember visiting Captain McGuire's ship when that early explorer an-

Schooner working through the ice

chored near Point Barrow in 1852. The whole burden of the
household seemed to fall on a very active, middle-aged woman
who bore a few tattoo lines on the back of one hand and three
tattoo bands on her chin, the middle band composed of four or
five lines being slightly broader than the other two.

Pushing on again, we came at nightfall to three more cabins,
one of them already occupied by Eskimos who had left Barrow
that same morning. We took over the second cabin, for in the
Arctic a traveler may use any empty dwelling he encounters provided that he leaves enough firewood for the next occupant. Our
neighbors told us that the *Karluk* or some other vessel had been
seen in the moving ice pack north of Point Barrow, but so far
from land that no one dared attempt to reach it.

An early start the next morning, October 12, brought us while
it was still daylight to Barrow, twelve miles south of the north-
ernmost point on the American continent. It contained at this
period an Eskimo settlement of 300 to 400 inhabitants, a government school and post office run by a Presbyterian missionary and
his wife, and a trading post operated by Charles Brower, an ex-

seaman who had settled here a quarter of a century before, married a woman of the village, and established himself as its leading resident. Brower confirmed the report that a vessel resembling the *Karluk* had drifted past Point Barrow. And he gave us other news. Our two schooners, the *Alaska* and the *Mary Sachs,* had found shelter in Camden Bay, halfway between Point Barrow and the Mackenzie River delta. A few miles beyond them lay three more vessels that had also been blocked by the ice pack, the veteran whaling steamer *Belvedere* and two small schooners, the *Elvira* and the *Polar Bear.* Close to Barrow itself, the ice had pushed on shore a Norwegian four-masted barque named the *Transit,* which had here discharged its cargo and reloaded before heading southward. The vessel was wrecked beyond recovery, but its crew had managed to escape unharmed and take refuge in the village, where two of its officers had set up a rival trading post in the hope of salvaging some of their losses before leaving this ill-fated region at the close of winter. Brower added, somewhat to my dismay, that several of the local Eskimos accused me of being responsible for the *Transit's* disaster, because it was carrying half a dozen human skeletons which I had gathered in an old graveyard on our way north to the Arctic Ocean and transshipped at Barrow as we passed by, and undoubtedly it was the vengeful spirit-owners of these skeletons that had evoked the destructive ice pack. Happily the Norwegians themselves never quite accepted my guilt, for they refrained from laying any formal charge against me.

Trader Brower joyfully welcomed the arrival of our party, for now that we had been cut off from our main base on the *Karluk* we needed a rather substantial outfit to carry us the three hundred miles eastward to our base on the *Alaska* and *Mary Sachs,* and his was the only trading post in the region which could supply that outfit. He organized his workers the very next morning, and while one native was stitching us a new tent, a second assembling a stock of provisions, and a third scouring the village for sled dogs, Mrs. Brower and another Eskimo woman began to cut up reindeer skins to make us new clothing for the severe months of winter that lay just ahead. Luckily skins were plentiful, since the local Eskimos owned nearly 1500 semi-domesticated reindeer, about 300 of which they had slaughtered during the summer for meat and clothing. At this period the live animal was valued at $25; its hide from $2.50 upward depending on its size and quality; and a "slab" of sinew from its back, which furnished thread far superior to either linen or cotton for the sewing of fur, $1.00. It required from seven to eight reindeer skins to clothe a man completely, without including the strip of wolf or wolverine fur needed to border the hood and sleeves; and a wolverine skin large enough to trim three parkas sold for about $25. It thus cost the Eskimo who paid to have his clothes made (of course, almost none of them did) very nearly the same as it cost the American in the United States. On the other side of the ledger, the Eskimo was receiving at this time $15 for a white-fox fur, and for a good polar bear skin $60.

The weather was becoming steadily colder, and the thermometer fell occasionally to below zero Fahrenheit. A slight current along the shore near Brower's store kept open a narrow lane of water, on whose somber surface gleamed a few small ice floes. After the long silence of our sled journey it was pleasant to hear the lapping of waves and to watch the pebbles rolling to and fro on the beach. As I stood there one morning, the rising sun in the east and the moon in the west cast conflicting shadows on the white snow; and around the low sun gathered subdued tints of orange and gold, while the water assumed a strange greenish hue. An Eskimo passed me. He was dragging a kayak on top of a small sled, and he carried in his hand an old-fashioned sealing harpoon. Later I saw him return empty-handed; apparently no seal had raised its head above the surface within reach of his weapon. He was the last hunter in the village to use the harpoon of his forefathers; all others shot the seals with rifles and retrieved the carcasses that did not sink with a light grappling hook fastened to the end of a long pole or line. Nor was it only the harpooning of seals that was vanishing; other old crafts, even the building of sleds and umiaks, were falling into disuse, for natives who

24

The lane of open water

would not have hesitated in earlier days to build a sled or a boat with their own hands were now ordering these goods from Brower's embryonic factory.

I attended one evening a village dance that was being held in a rectangular, low-gabled dwelling similar in plan to the trapping cabins, but very much larger. It housed two families, and for that reason was fitted with two windows of seal intestine, one on each side of the door, while its long sleeping shelf had been divided into two halves by an upright partition. An orchestra of six men sat in a row in the middle of the floor, each man holding in his left hand a small tambourine; and around and above them, tightly packed, sat the audience, men, women, and children, many of them naked to the waist, since the room was so hot that it positively steamed.

As I squeezed through the doorway one of the drummers lightly tapped his tambourine and began to sing. The others joined in, and a middle-aged man, accepting their invitation, stepped forward and drew over his hands a pair of fur mittens. The drums then resounded with hard, clear strokes, the song rose loud, and the dancer, stiff in every muscle, waved his tense arms and beat a rapid tatoo on the floor with his right foot. Up and down, in and out, he weaved his arms, now darting them over his head, now crossing them, now shooting them forward with hoarse cries of *aiyá aiyá*. After perhaps two minutes the singing died away, whereupon the dancer, tossing his gloves in challenge to another man, retired to his place in the audience. His successor was either more ambitious or more jealous of his reputation, for he danced five times in succession, with resting intervals of one or two minutes only; and when at last he resumed his seat the perspiration was flowing in rivulets down his face and body and he seemed completely exhausted.

Other dancers followed, but their performances were equally strained and gymnastic and for that reason somewhat monotonous. Neither on this occasion nor later did I observe any mimetic dances such as I had witnessed three months earlier in Nome. There one King Island Eskimo had staged a regular ballet, which portrayed with amazing fidelity the fluttering efforts of a mother ptarmigan to lure an enemy away from the fledglings in her nest.

Brower's trading store stood on a narrow sandspit between the sea and a small lagoon whose frozen surface provided the villagers with a smooth and level playground. Here they played a kind of football, using a rag bundle slightly larger than a baseball. The games I witnessed were mere free-for-alls without any rules: the players kicked the ball, threw it, ran with it, and even tripped their adversaries without hesitation. They told me, however, that in earlier times when they used a ball of caribou hide sewed tightly around a bundle of fur, kicking alone was permissible and tripping definitely outlawed.

Inside Brower's store I watched two children play another game. They sat face to face on the floor, locked their right wrists, and pulled as hard as they could away from each other. Afterwards they locked their left wrists and pulled, then the thumbs

and the four fingers in turn. This was a very ancient winter pastime, as popular with adults as with children; for Arctic nights
are long, and even trivial distractions help the hours to pass more
quickly.

The children played also a few European games they had
learned at school, for more and more foreign elements were beginning to bore their way into the native life. Thus only a few
houses in the village were now built of upright logs like the trapping cabins, or possessed long entrance corridors made of logs
covered with snow blocks. The majority were frame dwellings
similar to Brower's home and store; and they were protected in
front by enclosed porches built either of frame or of rectangular
blocks of ice cut from the neighboring lagoon with handsaws or
crosscut saws. None of the younger women had tattooed their
chins, but each of them, whether married or single, wore a silver
or brass ring on the third finger of the left or right hand — it
seemed not to matter which. Likewise, none of the men had perforated their lower lips to hold the oval labret that had once been
fairly common; and the few who had pierced the corners of their
mouths for the small button-type labret generally left the holes
empty. Only the coiffure seemed to have resisted innovations.
The men still allowed their hair to tumble freely on all sides, although they now trimmed the crown with European scissors,
guided usually by a china bowl; and the women continued as in
earlier times to part their hair down the middle with their fingers,
then gather it into two braids which they often joined together
at the nape of the neck.

The days passed rather monotonously, and although our new
outfit was not yet ready, we began to chafe a little under the
forced inactivity. Stefansson, who sensed the unrest, then instructed Wilkins and me to return to the lake beyond Cape Halkett
and to lay in a store of fish until such time as he himself put in
an appearance, probably about November 7. With two Eskimos
and two dog teams, therefore, Wilkins and I started out on October 27 to retrace our steps eastward.

URING the fifteen days that
we had lingered at Barrow the coast to the eastward had become
a veritable hive of activity, for the trapping season was less than
three weeks away and it behoved every man to pre-empt a trapping ground and set his traps in position before the opening
day. Most of the Eskimos simply resumed possession of the cabins
they had built or occupied the winter before; but there were a
few who, dissatisfied with their luck the previous season, wanted
to try out new districts and new neighbors, even if it involved
the building of new homes. With a small population and a coast
line that stretched for several hundred miles such changes gave
little occasion for disputes or quarrels.

Two, or more rarely three, families agreed to settle at a certain
place together, partly for company, partly because they knew
there would be times when they needed each other's help. They
then divided the trapping area around their new home to a
radius of from five to seven miles, which was as far as a man
could patrol during the short days of midwinter; and one family
set its traps in the western part of the area, the other in the
eastern. Only when they settled on a narrow peninsula did they

work the entire circle: normally, they neglected the inland half of their territory in favor of the shore and offshore, because the foxes themselves seemed to prefer the sea ice in winter, a season in which they subsisted mainly on stranded whale carcasses and on scraps of meat left over by the wolves and polar bears.

Wilkins and I, then, anticipated an easy journey, knowing that every ten or fifteen miles there would be an Eskimo cabin in which we could find shelter if for any reason we preferred not to set up our tent. About an hour after leaving Barrow we halted for a moment to examine three or four ancient house mounds which rose in oval hummocks above the almost level plain; and our Eskimos anxiously warned us not to walk on top of the largest mound lest the *tornrak* or spirit that dwelt inside it should resent our curiosity and stir up a gale. We scrupulously heeded their warning, and for two days enjoyed fine weather; but then the malicious spirit caught up with us, sending an easterly blizzard to assault us right in the middle of Smith Bay, where our inaccurate chart had led us astray on the journey west. Only with the greatest difficulty did we manage to pitch our tent beside a small ice hummock and huddle inside, with the door tightly fastened behind us; our dogs we left to fend for themselves, curled up grimly in the lea of the tent, unfed, and still wearing their harnesses.

All night the whistling wind drove the snow before it, and the whirling flakes penetrating inside the tent covered our sleeping bags with a thick white quilt that seemed strangely warm and comfortable. It felt less comfortable in the morning when we dressed and lit the primus stove to make tea. Our two Eskimos were dispirited and afraid, remembering that only a few years before two white men and their Eskimo guide had lost their way in this treacherous bay and had frozen to death. However, a light breakfast raised their courage; and, clambering outdoors, we shoveled free the sled from underneath the snow, loaded it, and extricated the dogs, whose noses alone were visible above the deep drift. Wilkins marched in front to set the course, and the dogs, pointing their muzzles downward, bravely battled the gale be-

Arkuvak

hind him. For an hour we plodded heavily along. Then fortune smiled on us, guiding us to a fairly fresh sled trail, which, two hours later, long before we were expecting it, brought us to the eastern shore of the bay at Drew Point. There we found temporary shelter under a cutbank while we fed our gallant dogs, who had eaten nothing for forty-four hours.

Beyond Drew Point we came upon two rectangular tents of white drill, and near them a number of people flitting like shadows amid the drifting snow as they cheerfully struggled to build more comfortable dwellings of driftwood. We shouted a greeting as we trudged by, and pressing on, reached, just as darkness closed in, the three cabins at *Ukallik*, "Hare," that twenty-one days before had stood silent and empty. Now all three of them were occupied, two by single families, the third by two families comprising an elderly man, his wife, and their four-year-old girl, and a young couple with a baby that was just beginning to walk. Since their cabin was considerably larger than either of the other two we accepted their offer of hospitality and carried our sleeping bags inside, the more gladly because Wilkins' forehead and chin had been nipped by frostbite and my own nose had not emerged unscathed.

The blizzard raged all the next day, so that no one ventured to stir abroad except to visit one or another of the neighboring cabins. Arkuvak, our elderly host, spent the hours of daylight in fastening a line of bone sinkers to the bottom of his fish-net, one sinker for every fifteen meshes; and his wife, after patching our worn boots, made Wilkins a fur band to protect his frost-bitten forehead. She complained toward evening of a stomach-ache, whereupon the younger woman prescribed eleven drops from a bottle labeled "artificial essence of peppermint." Although I cannot define the precise virtues of this medicine I can honestly testify to its potency, because the patient soon became deeply engrossed in a game of cards to which the neighbors challenged our house, and she did not complain of her stomach again.

The third day also we lingered here, since the storm showed no signs of abating. About 10 A.M. our neighbors, who had discovered from a hand-copied calendar that it was Sunday, joined our two families in morning service; for more than an hour the adults prayed in turn and sang hymns, one of which had the familiar tune of "Abide with Me." They sang and prayed in Eskimo, of course, since none of them understood English; and they conducted the service very reverently, even though the four little children shuffled about a good deal and the dogs in the corridor howled mournfully in an uninvited chorus. Just how much of Christianity's real teaching they had grasped I could not know; but I observed that whereas our host had prayed aloud for more than ten minutes on the night of our arrival, on the second night his prayer was much shorter, and on this Sunday night, when we retired to bed, he omitted to pray at all, at least audibly. Perhaps he wished to remind us that in the Arctic, as in other parts of the world, even the most appreciated guest can quickly outstay his welcome.

The storm blew itself out the next morning, and, grateful but relieved, we proceeded on our way. About noon we passed a new settlement of three cabins, and a few minutes later waved to a man who was traveling closer inshore, and in the opposite direction. Then, at dusk, as we drew near two more cabins, we overtook a party consisting of three men, a woman carrying a tiny baby on her back, and a four-year-old child snugly wrapped in a reindeer hide on top of their sled. Both we and they sought refuge in the larger of the two cabins, which measured no more than 24 feet wide by 16 feet deep and was already occupied by six people.

After the first few minutes of confusion, however, it seemed to possess ample room for us all, probably because all along the back of the room, about 3 feet above the floor, there extended a wide shelf on which the inmates could sit during the day, dangling their legs over the front edge, and at night make their beds, thus freeing the space beneath for any guests.

Everyone was very cheerful, even our hostess, who like hostesses everywhere, bore the brunt of the invasion. Her husband brought in firewood for the stove whenever she needed it, and the other women aided her by inspecting and mending some of the clothing. Much to her delight, too, one of the men devoted most of the evening to her eight-year-old son, teaching him how to balance seven or eight short sticks on his nose and let them fall, one by one, into his mouth. Yet even with their assistance the poor woman had to cook and sew for several hours, and she was visibly worn out long before it was bedtime.

Matters went better in the morning, when she rose early and set about cooking another pile of scones or baking-powder biscuits to replace the pile that we had demolished the evening before. Someone brought in two primus stoves, and while she herself baked one batch in the oven of her wood-burning stove, and fried a second on top of it, the visiting lady fried a third batch over one of the primuses and boiled still more in a pail of lard over the second primus. This time we had enough and to spare, and did not need to supplement the biscuits with rice boiled in seal oil, as had been our misfortune the evening before. We finished off the meal, as usual, with copious cups of tea. Wilkins and I then loaded our sleds and moved off, leaving a few gifts to mark our appreciation; but the family that had arrived with us stayed on, having arranged to share this cabin all winter.

We had learned during our journey westward to Barrow that the carcasses of two bowhead whales lay stranded on the seashore, one on the west side of Cape Halkett, the other on the east side; and since whale meat is excellent dog food, Stefansson had instructed us to chop out about a thousand pounds of it, and to cache it in the vicinity where it would be available to our ex-

A half-breed girl

pedition at some future date. The task occupied us two days,
during which we lodged with the neighboring Eskimos who had
been our hosts a month earlier. Since that visit they had enlarged the smaller of their two cabins by building on a second
room at the back and opening up part of the intervening wall,
and it was this back room that they now turned over to us. We
occupied it alone the first night, but the next afternoon our old
stammering friend Angopcana arrived with his three women and
insisted on sharing the space with us. However, they were a merry
lot, especially the octogenarian lady who had visited McGuire's
ship. She laughed heartily when she saw Wilkins' frostbitten face,
and slyly remarked how sad she felt that so handsome a man
should now have lost all his good looks.

Lady McGuire, as we nicknamed her, was one of the few
original inhabitants of the Barrow district, most of whom had
been swept away by European-introduced diseases. Our own
two Eskimos were natives of Point Hope, four hundred miles to
the southwest, as were also three or four others we had encountered along the coast. Still others had once dwelt inland, in the
Colville River basin and elsewhere; they had been drawn to the

Barrow region by the decrease of the caribou in the interior, the abundance of white foxes on the coast, and the facilities there for trapping them and for selling their furs. In Barrow itself I had noticed three or four children who were obviously part white, not counting those of Brower himself and of his white cook Hobson; and here in the little settlement near Cape Halkett two young married women seemed also to be of mixed blood, judging from the pale skin and fair hair of the one, and the slender face and wavy hair of the other. Yet it was not easy to estimate the amount of white mixture that had taken place in this region, because the Eskimos are themselves rather light-skinned, especially in winter after they lose their summer tan.

There could be no doubt that Lady McGuire belonged to an earlier generation, because she never tied the end of her braid with a ribbon like the other women, but passed it through an ivory bead. Neither did she roll and smoke the cigarettes that had become fashionable with the younger people, but puffed on an old-style pipe. Smoking was not new in this part of the world, for it reached the Alaskan Eskimos from northeast Siberia at least two hundred years ago, long before any European vessels had visited the coast line north of Bering Strait. The early pipe, which was still being used by Lady McGuire and a few old men, possessed a bowl made from walrus ivory, a mouthpiece of the same material, and a long stem of willow that had been split, hollowed, and then lashed together again. The bowl was quite tiny, because only minute quantities of tobacco ever trickled over in trade from the Siberian shore. Whenever the supply ran out, the Eskimos could, and often did, substitute *kinikinik*, the dried leaf of the bearberry bush; but tastier still was the chopped-

Lady McGuire's pipe

34

up stem of the willow pipe itself after it had become thoroughly impregnated with nicotine. As soon as whaling ships penetrated to Arctic Alaska and brought inexhaustible quantities of tobacco the Eskimos replaced the ivory bowls of their pipes with empty brass cartridges that were more resistant to heat; or they bought pipes of white manufacture. A few were still more progressive; they learned from the white seamen to dispense with pipes altogether and to enjoy the full flavor of the tobacco by chewing it.

Old habits of thriftiness disappear very slowly, and it was not surprising that the Eskimos should be sparing not of tobacco only, but of tea. Young and old were avid drinkers of this beverage, which they brewed in the kettle itself, not in a separate pot, and considered hardly palatable unless it was quite black. After each meal, the housewife scrupulously returned to the kettle the residue in all the teacups, leaves as well as liquid, so that the next brew might be as strong as the previous one or even stronger. Sooner or later, of course, the kettle contained more leaves than water. When it reached that stage, she merely emptied it completely and started the brewing all over again.

One day's run from Cape Halkett brought us to the last of the winter trapping cabins, a small one built by our first acquaintance, Arksiatark, to replace the tent in which he had entertained us after we had landed from the *Karluk*. As we approached his new home over the snow-encrusted ice an excessive refraction of light such as occurs very frequently in polar regions raised the dwelling into the sky and magnified it to three times its proper size; at the same time a cutbank two miles away loomed as big as a mountain, although its real height did not exceed fifteen feet. Arksiatark himself was absent, having gone to the fishing lake fifteen miles away just a few days before, but his wife and three children greeted us cheerfully and invited us into their hut.

Here for the first time I saw a characteristic blubber-burning lamp — not the elongated platter of soapstone that the Eskimos used in pre-white days, but a replica of it in wood, tin-sheeted, that rested on two pegs driven into the middle of the front wall.

In shape and size it resembled one half of a folding omelet pan, or one of those mess tins that British soldiers used in World War I. A narrow wick of shredded moss that had been pinched up along its straight front edge trailed back into a pool of yellow oil which accumulated, drop by drop, from a slab of melting blubber impaled on a peg above it. When carefully trimmed, this lamp gave a flame equal perhaps to that of two candles, and emitted very little smoke. It contributed, also, an appreciable amount of heat—enough, when augmented by the warmth of eight human bodies, to melt some of the snow on the roof of the cabin and create a very noticeable leak, as I learned to my sorrow during the night. Such a thing could never have happened during the winter if Arksiatark had insulated his roof properly; but so anxious had he been to return to the fishing lake that he had covered its logs with only about half the usual thickness of turf. Every cabin, however well insulated, leaked heavily late in the spring under the warmth of the returning sun; and throughout the summer many were flooded with water, which changed to ice in the early fall. Before reoccupying them, therefore, their owners had to rip out the floor boards, chip away the ice or drain off the water, and set the boards in place again as evenly as the rough ground permitted.

Knowing that every large body of water in this region had its choice fishing spots, we hurried to the lake the next day so that Arksiatark might show us just where to set our nets; but he had drawn up his own nets and departed for the coast three hours before our arrival. Of the two families that remained at the lake, one—Kunarluark's—also departed for the coast two days later, leaving its domed tent barred with snow blocks to keep out marauding animals. Snow had drifted all around its base to a depth of nearly two feet, making it appear half-underground; and protecting its doorway was a short corridor of snow blocks, supported by a framework of willow sticks in the same manner as the tent itself. So much warmer and more comfortable did it seem than the huge rectangular tent we were occupying that we requisitioned it for ourselves. Its board door attached by leather hinges to the willow frame opened on a space 14 feet long, 10½ feet wide, and 4½ feet high, lit by a window of seal intestine sewn into the cloth roof. A flooring of boards covered the front half of the interior, and a matting of willow twigs the back half, where it kept the bed skins from touching the snow. Still in place on the left of the entrance was the stove, which the owners had not needed for their cabin on the coast. Even if they had, it would almost have been easier for them to fashion a new one from a few empty kerosene tins than to transport the old stove, two tins being enough to make the stove itself (or, if ovenless, only one), and two others the pipes. No great skill was needed. Indeed, every Eskimo along the coast could make one in half a day given only three simple tools: strong scissors to cut the metal, a pair of pliers to bend it, and an ordinary hammer to blunt its jagged edges and to flatten out the overlapping seams.

As soon as we had moved our bedding and cooking gear into the domed tent, Wilkins and I proceeded to set our fishing nets, while our two natives drove back to the coast for a sledload of firewood. The lake was a very shallow body of water that drained to the sea by a still shallower stream, and the latter had already frozen so deeply that the fish in the lagoon were completely land-locked. We first drew in the nets of our sole remaining neighbor, Arlook, who was leaving for the coast the next morning; then we set our own nets through the same holes, which were about twenty-five yards apart, and joined to one another beneath the ice by long cords that served to pull the nets under. Arlook, using three nets, had been catching each day nearly 100 fish, which he was storing in a lidless refrigerator made from four rectangular blocks of ice too high, and too slippery, for any dog to clamber over. Since we had two nets about the same length as his, we expected a daily catch of perhaps 50; but we averaged only 16 during the fortnight we kept them set, and only a few more when we set an extra net that Arlook had left behind. He had indeed warned us that our nets were too deep for so shallow a lake, and their mesh too fine; but I rather think the lake was becoming exhausted; or perhaps the fish were now lying more dormant, for they appear to move about very little during the greater part of the winter. Whatever the reason, our catch was hardly big enough to satisfy the hunger of our two dog teams, so that it was impossible to accumulate the surplus that Stefansson was counting on for his journey to Camden Bay.

Wilkins shot a white fox just after we had set our nets, and, not trusting the skill of our own Eskimos, he asked Arlook to skin it for him. Our neighbor set about the task under the light of a hurricane lantern, supplemented by an ingenious lamp made from a pan of whale oil in which floated the lid of a baking-powder tin slotted in the center for a cotton wick. First he washed off some of the blood that stained the animal's head and neck; then he began to skin it, starting at the mouth and rolling back the fur until it came away clear but inside out. After scraping off the flesh and fat that adhered to this underside he reversed the skin, stamped it vigorously in the dry snow outdoors to remove all the remaining bloodstains, and passed it to his wife to stitch up the bullet hole. When the sewing was finished he slit the legs and tail, stretched the fur over a long but narrow V-shaped frame to keep it from shrinking, and hung it up to dry. The entire operation occupied him two and a half hours. Incidentally, this was the standard method of skinning foxes, because it reduced to a minimum the danger of marring the fur with grease stains, which cannot be removed without chemicals.

Two weeks passed slowly by. Each day we examined our fish nets, roamed over the surrounding countryside during the short hours of daylight looking for ptarmigan and other game, and waited for Stefansson. He arrived at last on November 21, along with McConnell and a fifteen-year-old half-breed, Alfred ("Brick") Hobson, the son of Brower's cook. In a midnight discussion immediately following his arrival Stefansson told me that he intended to push on without delay in order to join the rest of our expedition in Camden Bay, but that I was to stay behind with Arksiatark's family for at least part of the winter, learning the Eskimo language and picking up whatever information I could on Eskimo customs and folklore. Brick Hobson would stay with me as my interpreter, at a salary of $15 a month; but he was to be as free as Arksiatark and the other Eskimos to set his steel traps and catch whatever foxes luck brought in his way. Cached on top of a platform on the western side of Cape Halkett I would find two hundred pounds of rice, sugar, macaroni, and other foods; and I could keep our smallest sled and six dogs. At Christmas, or as soon as possible afterward, a party from Camden Bay would bring me a further supply of food so that I might remain in this area until spring.

The next morning we pulled up the fish nets and returned to the coast, where we pitched our tents beside Arksiatark's cabin, now occupied also by Arlook, who proved to be his brother-in-law. Two days later Stefansson, Wilkins, McConnell, and one of our Point Hope Eskimos departed eastward, their two sleds heavily laden with two hundred pounds of whale meat and four hundred frozen fish that they had purchased from Arlook. I was left behind with Brick Hobson. With us too remained Jimmy, one of our Point Hope Eskimos, who had requested his discharge from the expedition so that he too might trap in this vicinity. To be sure, he possessed no traps of his own, but he expected to borrow a few from Arlook, paying for them later with a proportion of his catch.

A MATCH flared suddenly in the dark cabin, and the shavings of dry cottonwood that caught the flame lit up the long, lean features of my host Arksiatark. He was kneeling on the edge of the sleeping skins, naked from the waist upward, and, below, covered with a pair of caribou-skin breeches with the fur side inward. His hair, which his wife had recently trimmed with a pair of scissors and a bowl, shone like a circular dish of polished jet, and his eyes were two little beads of jet glowing above a Roman nose and jutting cheek bones the color of old ivory. The long face with its hollow cheeks and pointed chin matched the rest of his body, which tapered downward from the broad shoulders, swelled a trifle at the hips, then trailed away into seemingly endless limbs with the feet somewhere in the distance.

As soon as the fire in the stove had well started he glanced around. Side by side on the floor, under caribou robes, were stretched out ten figures, their feet against the back wall and their heads pillowed on their fur parkas in a long row across the middle of the room. Nearest him lay his nine-year-old daughter Seeluk, whose left arm gently encircled her baby brother Toopin; and beyond, hard against the wall, slept his wife Kavik, whose gaunt face seemed to lose none of its sourness even in repose. On his other side was the elder daughter Cookpuck, named after the great Colville River on whose banks she had first opened her eyes. That had been a day of extreme disappointment for the mother, who had hoped for a boy; and she would have stifled the baby on the day of its birth had she not been afraid of her husband, who firmly opposed infanticide even though his people had practiced it from time immemorial. Ever since, she had entertained a deep dislike for the child, and neglected it as much as she dared, with the result that at the age of twelve Cookpuck's grave face had lost all the merriment of other children, and her sad eyes seemed always to wonder what the world still kept in store for her, and to anticipate the worst rather than the best.

These four made up Arksiatark's immediate family, with the exception of his eighteen-year-old son Itarklik, who had settled down temporarily with another family on the western side of Cape Halkett so that he might set his fox traps nearer to the whale carcasses. However, Arlook and his wife Capcana, Arksiatark's sister, were sharing the cabin for the winter; and at this moment their daughter Imeroon slumbered under the same robe with her older cousin Cookpuck, while the parents lay just beyond, snuggling between them a nine-month-old baby.

The little cabin, built for one family only, seemed to shrink together with this litter of eight humans; and yet two more persons, Brick and Jimmy, had managed to squeeze into the three feet of space between Arlook and the far wall, while I lay across their heads just inside the doorway. Little wonder, therefore, that Arksiatark's inquiring glance gave way to an impatient frown. He jerked on his buttonless double parka, the inner of

Brick

mountain-sheep skin with the fur against his body, the outer of white drill — or of drill that had been white nine months before when it first left Brower's store. (Each parka had a hood or capote that could be drawn over the head like a bonnet, and the edge of the drill capote was trimmed with soft brown wolverine fur to protect the forehead, cheeks, and chin.) He pulled up both hoods, drew on his socks and boots of caribou fur (the boots, but not the socks, were soled with sealskin), clapped his hand to his hip to make certain of his hunting knife, then, snatching up his mittens, leaned over me, pushed back the door and stepped outside. It was eight o'clock in the morning, and the first glimmer of dawn would not appear for at least an hour; yet, breakfastless, he was going off to visit his fox traps, and would return only at mid-afternoon, when the short winter daylight was fading again into night. He had finished laying his traps the day before the opening of the official season — that period from mid-November to the end of March when a skillful trapper might hope to kill as many as fifty white foxes and perhaps two or three white bears. With Brower paying $15 apiece for the fox skins, he anticipated that the income from his four months' trapping would purchase not only all his necessities for the coming year, but a number of luxuries beside.

Arlook emerged from his sleeping bag a few minutes later, and, without disturbing the others, departed to inspect his own traps, which were scattered along the coast in a direction opposite to Arksiatark's. I followed him outdoors, not because I had anywhere to go, but to escape the stifling atmosphere of the nearly airtight room. The moon was still high in the west, flooding the landscape with its soft light. Strictly speaking there was no landscape, only a white brightness all around, faintly broken at my feet by some withered blades of grass that protruded through the all-pervading snow. The frozen sea a few yards distant merged indistinguishably with the land. No tree or hill caught my wandering eye, no mound even except the white outline of the cabin behind me, whose black, yawning entrance seemed like the opening to another world. It was a land of silence and desolation that stretched unbroken to the far horizon. Yet the air was crisp and clear, with a freshness in its icy breath that tingled the veins and stirred every muscle into activity. The impulse to run was irresistible.

The only person who was stirring when I re-entered the cabin was Mrs. Arksiatark, who had pulled on her combination trousers and socks and was busily preparing the breakfast. She had brought in from the platform eight or nine frozen whitefish, each a foot long, and laid them against the front wall to thaw out. Now from the corner she produced an enamel wash basin into which she poured four cupfuls of flour, a bare quarter teaspoonful of baking powder, and just enough water to make a batter. She mixed the dough with her hands, then kneaded it into little flat biscuits, which she slapped on the top and side of her small ovenless stove. The fire roared merrily, the drops of perspiration that dripped from her face and body spluttered on the hot iron, and from time to time she hitched up her drooping trousers lest they should slip about her knees. Meanwhile the biscuits on the top of the stove began to smoke, and those on the side to drop,

Eskimo child

one by one, to the floor; but as fast as they dropped she slapped them back on their uncooked faces. Finally all were baked and safely deposited again in the wash basin under the stove. She then filled the kettle with cold water, poured into it a teaspoonful of fresh "Gunpowder tea" (so read the label), and placed it on top of the stove to boil.

"Brick, Jimmy," she called in Eskimo. "Breakfast is ready; get up and eat."

The children tucked themselves away at the back of the cabin to eat their breakfast, while the rest of us sat in a circle near the stove and munched tender parings of raw, frozen fish, which we sliced with our knives as one slices an apple. One fish apiece was our allotted ration, and we munched noisily, for to eat in silence, my companions believed, was to eat like a thief. And because fish by itself is somewhat dry, between each mouthful we dipped our fingers into a bowl of rancid seal oil that Mrs. Arksiatark set in our midst. As soon as we had finished this course she passed around the skin of a ptarmigan so that we might wipe our greasy faces and hands; and she counted out for each of us two of her biscuits, *mookpaurat,* "food that you turn over in baking just as you turn over the pages of a book." That, at least, was their official name; but Jimmy and Brick secretly called her variety *cacocktat:* "food that cracks between your teeth like bone." To be sure, she was not as openhanded as Mrs. Arlook, and she lacked her sister-in-law's skill in preparing foreign foods; yet her husband considered her an excellent housewife, a proper mate for a hunter whose days so often alternated between plenty and want. She was certainly generous enough with her tea, but of course it was easy to replenish the water from the snow outside, and any leaves that inadvertently dropped into the cups would later find their way back into the kettle.

Dawn was breaking as we finished our breakfast, the dawn which for four hours in midwinter never ceased to promise day, but which faded away without ever fulfilling the promise. I went off with Brick to watch him set a line of fox traps, while Jimmy, who had borrowed four traps from Arlook, sauntered away in another direction to lay down his. Brick planted his first trap about five miles from the cabin, after first smearing it with a few drops of redolent "castor" that he had brought from Barrow; and he then set two others within a radius of perhaps a mile. By that time the bright glow in the sky had passed the south meridian and was setting swiftly westward. We therefore turned our steps homeward, and on the way discovered a steel trap that Arlook had set on the bank of a small river. The trap itself was buried out of sight beneath the snow, but scattered around it were chips of frozen whale blubber, and one end of the stick to which its chain was fastened rested on an upturned clod of earth black enough to attract any fox that happened to be wandering in the vicinity. Less than a mile from the cabin we stumbled on another trap, this one a deadfall made of logs, with a slab of whale blubber impaled on its wooden trigger. I suspect that it too had been set by Arlook, because he was always experimenting, and, in fact, had already caught one fox near the fishing lake with an ingeniously contrived noose.

It was dark when we reached the cabin, guided home by the pale glow from its skylight. Arksiatark and Arlook had preceded us, and Jimmy arrived a few minutes later, bringing a fox from one of Arlook's traps that its owner had not found time to visit. Although the others had finished eating, Mrs. Arksiatark immediately set some frozen fish and biscuits before us, and poured us out some tea; for she knew that a woman should never keep her men-folk waiting for a meal when they came in from their trap lines or from hunting. Each of us in turn then related the day's adventures, especially the number of tracks that he had seen and the direction in which their makers were traveling. By the time this topic was exhausted Arlook's fox, which had been thawing out near the stove, was ready for skinning. He commenced the operation without delay, while Arksiatark, tired from the day's exertions, lay back on the bed skins and chanted dance-songs, beating the time with his hand. His wife stretched out beside him and added her voice to make a duet; the children played with their dolls at the back of the cabin; and Jimmy, with a pack of cards that he produced from an old knapsack, tried to teach the rest of us a new kind of poker he had learned at Point Hope. Slowly the evening dragged on, and several members of the household crawled inside their sleeping bags before Arlook finally hung up his fox fur and his wife extinguished the lamp. The cabin and all its inmates instantly vanished in the intense darkness, and the silence of the Arctic night closed in around us, a leaden, oppressive, almost pulsating silence that was broken only by the occasional snore of some sleeper, or by the scratching of a dog in the snow outside.

Two days later Arlook complained that his chest was paining him, whereupon his wife, much alarmed, heated a pan of water, and, after a short prayer, washed the upper part of his body. Mrs. Arksiatark then repeated the prayer and dried him, using the all-purpose family towel. He remained in the cabin all day, and at evening stripped to the waist again and gave himself a kind of sweat bath by sitting as close to the stove as he could and drinking cupful after cupful of very hot tea. Although the pain persisted for several days, forcing him to neglect his trap line, he did not repeat the treatment, probably because he anticipated that the prayers uttered by his women-folk would of themselves bring about a cure.

One must remember that these people were inland Eskimos who had scarcely come into contact with civilization. Mrs. Arksiatark had never traveled even the short distance to Barrow; and her husband had visited that village only once in his forty or fifty years. Neither had ever seen the inside of a church or heard a missionary's sermon. They knew no more of Christianity than the half-dozen hymns and prayers that had filtered through to them from their neighbors, together with a prohibition against performing any kind of work on Sundays, even sewing a patch on a worn mitten. It was therefore only natural that they should interpret these outward expressions of Christianity in the light of their earlier beliefs, and should look upon the prayers and hymns and prohibitions of the immigrant religion as in no way different from the incantations and taboos that had been handed down to them from their forefathers, or enjoined by some old-time medicine man. They merely surmised that the new rituals must be more effective than the old ones, since the white man was acquainted with many things that were beyond the Eskimos' knowledge. I myself could only reflect that even this faint glimmer of the Christian faith was an improvement on their earlier outlook, because it strengthened their psychological defenses against the hostile and often gruesome creatures with which their imaginations continued to people the universe, and it lessened the fear of the supernatural and the unknown that so often obsessed their waking hours.

It was in fact only a few days after Arlook became ill that this fear of the supernatural (to them it was not supernatural) rose so openly to the surface that even I could feel its intensity. Arksiatark, who had left as usual before daylight to make the round of his trap line, returned unexpectedly an hour before dark and threw a dead white fox onto the floor just inside the cabin door. Never a talkative man, he seemed on this occasion even moodier than usual, and paid no attention to his wife and children as he took his customary place on the bed skins. Nor did he speak throughout supper, when simultaneously we plunged our spoons into the pot of rice that his wife set in front of us, then continued the meal at a more leisurely pace with a frozen fish apiece and some biscuits. Later, however, when some of us were absorbed in a card game, he dropped a remark that made the players lay down their cards and look at him with anxious faces. After a moment of silence he went on talking. I understood only a

The evening meal

few words of what he was saying, but Brick translated for me afterward. This was the gist of his narrative.

"I was crossing over from that little island where we stored our blubber last spring; for it was there I found the fox, caught in the trap by its left hind leg. I was walking along, headed for the promontory, when my protecting spirit made me look seaward, and I saw a black speck moving to and fro among the broken ice cakes. At first I thought it was another hunter, and wondered why he had gone so far out to sea, for there is no open water any longer and no hope of shooting more seals; but just as I had changed my course to meet him I saw another black speck, and a third, all moving backward and forward with the first. Then I knew it was a *cocogark* lying on its back and waving its ten legs in the air to attract attention. I didn't dare go closer, but hurried as fast as I could to the mainland; and evidently it didn't see me, for when I reached the shore it had disappeared."

No one said anything for a few minutes, but his wife rose and, closing the door a little tighter, trimmed the lamp and put a few more sticks of wood in the stove; for light and fire, they believed, were the surest protections against the unknown dangers of the outside world. She then advised her husband to keep away from the island in the hope that the monster would presently depart elsewhere. And Jimmy ventured the remark:

"I did not know there were any of those bears in this district. It was a *cocogark* that killed my cousin two summers ago. We had gone out in our kayaks to look for seals when a huge dark paw seized the stern of his boat and dragged him under the water. I paddled back to the place the next day, but could find only his empty kayak."

Arksiatark was not the man to take any unnecessary chances. He had been told too many stories about this monster — or monsters, for most natives believed there were several of them. Only two months before his relative Kunarluark had heard something swimming beneath his sled when he was traveling along the coast from Cape Smythe. He left the trail and moved inshore; and barely had he reached the land when a *cocogark* crashed its head through the spot he had just abandoned. Luckily the ice was so thin that the monster was unable to climb out and attack him, but, after remaining at the surface for a minute, slowly sank from sight again. Kunarluark had described the incident to Arksiatark after joining the latter at the fishing lake; and now Arksiatark himself had seen the monster. So for a few days he heeded his wife's advice and stayed away from the island, as did all the rest of us. Then, when nothing further happened, he cautiously resumed his trapping in that direction.

One day followed another rather monotonously as we issued each morning from our tiny house, isolated amid the infinite waste of ice and snow, and four or five hours later holed ourselves up in it again. I did not always join Brick in making the round of his trap line. Occasionally I stayed at home to saw up some of the stranded logs for firewood, split them into small billets, and pile them in the corridor. At other times I wandered off alone to look for ptarmigan, which feed all winter on the dry seeds of the grasses that raise their heads above the snow. Only once or twice was my rifle successful, because, though the ptarmigan moved about in small flocks, their white bodies blended so

Mrs. Arlook and her baby

perfectly with the white landscape that they were scarcely visible, even when they were no farther away than twenty or thirty yards. I might have been luckier with a shotgun, but that weapon would have been of little use against any polar bear that I was always hoping to encounter — whether wisely or not I do not know. So my hunting was rather unprofitable. Yet it served one useful purpose. It provided the stimulus that carried me out of doors into the fresh air, and forced me to take the exercise I needed so greatly after spending twenty hours in the stuffy and at times overheated cabin.

Living in such close proximity to the Eskimos I could not fail to be vaguely conscious of a tension in the atmosphere for which at the beginning I could find no reason. It was true that the cabin was far too small for us all, and that no one was really comfortable during the evening hours when we all gathered inside it; but Eskimos are accustomed to narrow quarters in winter, and the trouble here seemed to lie deeper. A casual remark by Brick one day suggested the true explanation, which was confirmed by later events.

Arlook's wife was a hunchback deeply conscious of her infirmity, although she tried to cloak her sensitiveness under a mask of gaiety. She knew that other Eskimos pitied her; but she knew also that many who pitied her harbored at the same time a lurking fear lest her infirmity might have given her special powers of witchcraft, which sooner or later she might be tempted to employ against some neighbor. In the quiet of her home she seemed to be a devoted wife and mother, inclined to spoil both her daughter Imeroon and the baby that slept each night in her arms. Her husband she trusted completely, for he never quarreled with anyone, but in his quiet efficient way always kept her supplied with firewood and with ice to melt for drinking water; indeed, if she were very tired, he would himself cook the meals, or scrape a hide to patch the children's clothing. Neither did she fear her brother Arksiatark with whom she had lived from childhood. What she did dread, apparently, was the jealousy of Mrs. Arksiatark, who seemed to resent her skill in cooking rice and biscuits and other

Imeroon

imported foods, and also her proficiency with the hand sewing machine. The older woman might rightfully claim to be the mistress of this one-room cabin which her husband had built with his own hands; but even to my unprejudiced eyes she went out of her way to assert her position. No wonder, then, that Mrs. Arlook often lapsed into silence and seemed a little uneasy.

I sensed the tension one noon when I was revising some folk tales and working out the grammar of a few Eskimo sentences that I had recorded the evening before. The two women sat against the walls on opposite sides of me, busily scraping caribou hides from which to make new clothing; and while Mrs. Arlook's baby rolled contentedly among the bed skins, her sister-in-law's little boy was playing with his mother's workbag. After a time I laid down my pencil and went outside to bring in a few sticks of firewood; and at the entrance to the corridor I paused a moment to watch the three little girls, who were juggling with a pair of fox paws they had substituted for the pebbles now frozen beneath the snow. Little Cookpuck followed me indoors, bringing a chunk of ice for the cooking pot; and as she turned, she hoisted her baby brother on to her back underneath her fur parka and carried him out to play in the snow. Presently I heard shouts and laughter, and recognized the refrain of a hide-and-seek song:

> Heads together, heads together,
> Stand with your heads together.
> She is hiding beyond the brook,
> She is hiding beyond the brook.
> Let us look for her. Come.

Mrs. Arksiatark heard the shouts also. She looked over at her sister-in-law, snapped out two or three words which I did not understand, and moved quickly toward the door.

"Please send Imeroon in also," said the younger woman.

"Cookpuck, Imeroon, come in at once," Mrs. Arksiatark called from the mouth of the corridor.

The two children followed her inside, Imeroon with a slight pout on her face. They sat cross-legged side by side under the skylight, and the younger girl proceeded to dress a doll under her mother's direction while Cookpuck mended her little brother's worn suit, which was a combination garment with shirt, trousers, boots, and mittens all joined into one. She sewed up the rents under each armpit, and replaced the old soles, worn to the thinness of paper, with a new pair that she deftly puckered at heels and toes by means of her thumbnail. Last of all she patched a hole in one mitten and handed the garment to her mother.

Mrs. Arksiatark examined it closely. The ends of the sinew thread must have been neatly hidden, and the stitches firmly and evenly spaced, for she found nothing to criticize. Laying the garment aside, she pushed over to the girl the half-dressed caribou hide that she had been scraping and told her to continue the work. Then, turning her back, she rummaged in her marmot-skin workbag, drew out some long strands of colored wool, tied their ends to a nail on the wall, and began to plait a girdle.

Presently Imeroon turned to Mrs. Arlook and said, handing her the doll:

"It is finished, mother. May I go out again?"

"No, little Imeroon," answered the mother gently. "It is not quite finished. Look." And she pointed to something at the neck.

The child took back the doll with a sigh and for a few minutes there was silence. Then her mother laid aside her own work, and, going over to the front wall, patted down the lamp wick.

"Cookpuck," she said. "Bring some blubber into the corridor."

Cookpuck glanced quickly at Mrs. Arksiatark and slipped out of the door like a squirrel. As soon as she had disappeared Mrs. Arlook turned to her own daughter and said:

"Run out and play now, little Imeroon. It will soon be dark."

Then, happy at the success of her strategy, she resumed her seat on the floor, gripped between her legs the hide that Cookpuck had been dressing, and, pulling it taut with her left hand, vigorously attacked it with the iron-headed scraper she held in her right.

The episode ended there, but the tension remained unrelieved,

Cookpuck the patient

Arlook's screw driver

for neither in the Arctic nor elsewhere can human beings ever transform themselves into ants and submerge their individualities in a general group consciousness. During the long mild days of summer, when the Eskimos roamed hither and yon to fish and hunt, a man (or woman) could relieve his pent-up emotions by wandering off alone for several hours or even days; but in winter, during eighteen of the day's twenty-four hours, the darkness and the cold inevitably confined him inside his tiny hut, where he was constantly brushing shoulders with the other inmates or stumbling over their outstretched legs. There were no mystery books to drug his mind, even had he been literate; no radios to titillate his ears, for none had yet reached the Arctic. At large settlements like Barrow he might forget his domestic irritations in a round of community games and dances, and in frequent visits to welcoming neighbors; but these recreations were not possible in the isolated trapping cabins. There the confinement and loneliness weighed heavily on the Eskimos, despite their habitual cheerfulness and patience. Both sexes felt the strain, the women, I thought, more than the men, who obtained at least temporary alleviation each day when they patrolled their trap lines. In earlier years the tension had sometimes given rise to bitter enmities that seethed unnoticed beneath the outwardly placid surface until they erupted suddenly in violent explosions. Arlook himself had witnessed such an explosion during his youth:

it left one native lifeless on the ground with a knife wound in his stomach, and his aggressor mortally wounded by a bullet in his back.

About noon some days later a fresh breeze sprang up from the eastward, and by night the drifting snow was lashing our membrane window like heavy rain beating against a pane of glass. The blizzard lasted two days, during which no one ventured to wander outdoors, not even the trappers. Brick and Jimmy whiled away the hours at cards, or competed with each other in the string game called cat's cradles; but Arksiatark used the enforced leisure to plane two small boards and mortice them together to form a snow shovel. He asked Arlook, who was an unusually skillful mechanic, to trim down a strip of whale rib and shape it into a cutting edge for the shovel, whereupon the latter proceeded to overhaul his own tool bag and to sharpen his saw and plane. Seeing me peek curiously into the bag, which was a long, oval pouch made from the whole skin of a seal, he spilled out its contents for my inspection. They consisted of an odd assortment of knives, files, drills, fragments of iron and bone, and other articles, some European, some Eskimo; but what most caught my eye was an ingenious screw driver, or rather a battery of screw drivers, that he himself had devised for taking to pieces his 30.30 Winchester rifle.

It required only this blizzard to bring to a head the universal dissatisfaction with the meagerness of our home. There was no room for the men to work, or the women to cook and sew; for no one could move a foot without bumping into someone else and endangering the stove and stovepipes. Something had to be done, and that quickly. We decided, therefore, that Jimmy, Brick, and I, with two sleds and dog teams, would cross the bay to the far side of Cape Halkett to bring back the provisions that Stefansson had cached there for me; and while we were absent Arlook and Arksiatark would build on a second room, so that each family might have living quarters of its own.

I T WAS still dark when we harnessed our dogs, but a magnificent auroral arc, green and orange and red, stretched across the sky from northwest to southeast almost through the zenith. It was broadest and brightest in the middle, but the two ends, neither of which quite touched the horizon, quivered and gleamed like the reflection of the rising sun in a gently undulating sea. The air was calm and clear, and our nearly empty sleds skimmed lightly over the hard-packed snow, leaving very little trace of their passage. In less than four hours we crossed the bay and sighted a post on the eastern shore line of Cape Halkett that marked the short cut across its isthmus; and without difficulty we picked up the corresponding post on the western shore. Thence a well-marked trail brought us, soon after dark, to our destination — two now familiar cabins, one, inhabited by the family of Kunarluark, whose tent Wilkins and I had occupied at the fishing lake, the other and larger one, by the stammering Angopcana and his women-folk.

Jimmy carried his sleeping bag into the smaller cabin, while Brick and I found a warm welcome in Angopcana's cozy home,

58

which was luxuriously lighted by three lamps, two of Eskimo type, platter-shape, the third a glass table lamp which they had purchased at Brower's store; for with two whale carcasses in the vicinity they could count on abundant blubber to supply the necessary oil. Soon we were dining on cold boiled brant, of which they had shot about two dozen in the fall just before the birds migrated southward.

Although Wilkins and I had stayed with this household a few weeks before, and I visited it twice again before the winter ended, I never did succeed in untangling all the family relationships. Gay old Lady McGuire was either the mother or the mother-in-law of Angopcana, and the blind lady, the mistress of the house, his wife. The latter seemed fairly cheerful despite her affliction; and it was pleasant to observe the respect which everyone paid her, and her own brave efforts to help out with the family tasks. Then there were the partly paralyzed woman and her husband, who must have been their close relatives; and the housekeeper and her husband Assuark, the latter a brother of Brower's wife and a native originally of Cape Prince of Wales, the eastern bulwark of Bering Strait. Finally, there was a second brother of Mrs. Brower, a seemingly unattached man named Amarcook, "Two Wolves," who in his own small world was a distinguished artist. Lying on his back on the sleeping bench, he had decorated the ceiling of this house with clever pencil sketches of caribou and other animals, just as a much greater artist in a much more sophisticated world had decorated the ceiling of the Sistine Chapel. I gave him paper and a pencil, with the promise of a liberal credit note on his brother-in-law's store at Barrow if he would draw similar sketches for me; and he spent the greater part of the evening in artistic endeavors that were very profitable to himself, and no less satisfactory to me. Two permanent members of Angopcana's elastic household, his son Ikpik and pretty daughter-in-law Aiva, were not present on this occasion, having gone off two or three days before to visit some neighbors along the coast.

Everyone in the little settlement was in good spirits, for the

Two Wolves' drawing of a summer camp

men had been unusually lucky during these first three weeks
of the trapping season, probably because they were living so close
to the whale carcasses. Arksiatark's son Itarklik, who was staying
with Kunarluark, headed the list with twenty-six foxes; but Ikpik
and another man were trailing him closely, and Ikpik had shot
a large polar bear whose hide was worth at least four fox skins.
Even the lady housekeeper had caught the fever and set two or
three traps on her own account, close enough to the cabin so that
she could visit them each day after breakfast and yet return in

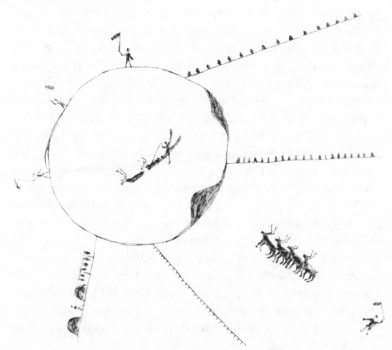

Two Wolves' sketch of a caribou hunt

time to prepare the evening meal. I did not inquire whether she had actually caught any foxes; but if she had, they were her exclusive property, to sell or not as she thought fit. Such was not the case with Arlook's and Arksiatark's daughters, who also could claim some fox traps that their fathers had set in their names; but their ownership was purely nominal, because they were much too young to tend the traps themselves.

As I sat on the wide sleeping bench and watched my artist friend Two Wolves execute his drawings on the sheets of paper, I puzzled over a number of seemingly useless wooden pegs that had been plugged into the ceiling above my head. But at bedtime one of the men transferred these pegs to a row of holes drilled into the thick beam that ran from wall to wall under the bench's front edge, where they sloped outward and slightly upward. He then rested on them a long board, which he covered with various clothes and bags. A few minutes later seven black heads in addition to my own lined up along this improvised bolster, which was so comfortable that I wondered why no other cabin had imitated the device.

The next morning Brick and I, with Jimmy's help, loaded our stores on the sleds in preparation for the return journey, then visited our neighbor Kunarluark, who had invited us to his cabin for a midday snack of biscuits and tea. The blind Mrs. Angopcana had preceded us there; she was sitting on the floor to one side, industriously making a pair of boots by stitching soles of mountain-sheep fur to uppers of caribou fur; and although she had only her touch to guide her the sewing on these boots was flawless. I discovered, after our morning tea, that she was an expert also at cat's cradles, a pastime that seemed extremely popular everywhere along this coast. With her single loop of string she could produce an amazing variety of fanciful birds and animals, and of people engaged in different pursuits. Some of the figures would dance for her, or race from one hand to the other; and as they ran she chanted different refrains that brought tears of laughter to the eyes of her listeners. She taught me how to make two figures I had not seen before, but warned me never to

61

Angopcana wearing his labrets

play the game after two stars named Agrook make their appearance in the sky just before the long days of summer. Then she put away her string; the brightness that had lighted up her face gave way to an expression of patient resignation, and, rising to her feet, she allowed Kunarluark's wife to lead her back to her own cabin, whither we followed her shortly after.

One by one the men returned from their trap lines, and we gathered in a circle for the evening meal. No sooner had we finished eating and moved back to our places than the artist began to narrate an old folk tale describing the manifold trials a brave hunter endured to rescue his wife, who had been abducted by men of a faraway village. The tale went on and on for more than two hours; yet the interest of the listeners never flagged for a moment, first one, then another, interrupting with comments and questions right to the very end. They told me that every large settlement in Arctic Alaska possessed one or more raconteurs like my artist who provided their fellow-villagers with agreeable but unpaid entertainment during the long dark evenings of winter; also that some of the stories were so long that they required three and even four evenings for the telling.

I suspect that either Kunarluark or one of the other Eskimos had quietly hinted that there were too many trappers in this locality, for at bedtime Arksiatark's son announced quite suddenly that he intended to take up his traps before daybreak and return with us to his father's home.

We rose about the same time as usual, but our warmhearted housekeeper refused to serve breakfast until she had filled our thermos with tea and baked some extra biscuits for our lunch. This delayed our start considerably, and with our heavily laden sleds we did not reach the post on the eastern side of Cape Halkett until well on in the afternoon. Already we had halted once to drain our thermos, but at this post my companions, afflicted with a seemingly insatiable thirst, insisted on stopping again so that they might light the primus and boil more tea. It is true that the sky was clear and comparatively calm; that the dogs could follow our earlier and still unobliterated trail; and that even if they strayed from it we ourselves knew approximately the right direction, and could guide ourselves by the stars. Nevertheless, being still somewhat of a novice in sled travel, I could not escape a certain uneasiness, knowing that the wide Harrison Bay ahead of us was completely devoid of landmarks, and that a dense fog could spring up very rapidly. Even if the atmosphere remained clear I foresaw no pleasure in stumbling over the pathless wastes of the frozen sea with no light but the stars and the aurora above us and their pallid reflections in the snow at our feet. Fortunately my misgivings were needless. About eight o'clock in the evening we sighted the glow of Arksiatark's skylight on the far side of the bay and knew that we had reached our destination.

During our absence Arlook and Arksiatark had fulfilled their promise to build a new room, but they had neither insulated it nor attached it to the original cabin. These operations had now to be postponed for a time, because the day following our return was a Sunday, when even sewing was prohibited; and on Monday the men considered it necessary to revisit their traps. Immediately after breakfast on Tuesday, however, everyone turned out with shovels and mattocks, and while two of us hacked up the turf from the frozen ground, others piled it against the walls and on the roof of the new room and banked it firmly with snow, taking care not to block the two holes for the skylight and the stovepipe. Arlook and Arksiatark, meanwhile, joined its roof to the roof of the old cabin, tossed out through the open skylight the turf insulation of the intervening wall, and sawed through this wall to make a common passage. At this stage we adjourned for supper, for it was long after dark; and we appeased our hunger with two foxes that Cookpuck had boiled in a cauldron over an open fire in the snow while her mother was making biscuits and tea indoors. It was then an easy matter for us to lay a floor in the room by passing the boards down through the skylight; and while Arlook set up the stove and lit a fire, his wife brought out her sewing machine and stitched a "windowpane" from seal intestines. By that time it was so late that her husband postponed framing the pane in the skylight and building a sleeping bench until another day. Instead, he and his family moved their bedskins into the new quarters and accepted Jimmy and Itarklik as their guests, while Brick and I continued to share the old room with Arksiatark's household.

It was shortly after we had enlarged the dwelling that, returning home somewhat late one evening, I found all the trappers sitting around a bowl of unadulterated blubber. They opened up the circle to make a place for me and courteously invited me to share their repast; but just as courteously I declined, having already made several unsuccessful attempts to slither the oily tidbits down my throat. Mrs. Arksiatark looked troubled, and solicitously handed me one of her tooth-cracking biscuits coated with a tiny hillock of cold boiled rice that she had held back from breakfast; and with this more familiar food I tried to dull

the appetite aroused by five hours of wandering outdoors in sub-zero temperatures. Happily for me, the meal proved to be only a prelude to supper, not the supper itself. An hour later she served us a dish of unseasoned oatmeal, more brittle biscuits, and some tea.

"Hunger provides the sauce"

Brick had complained to me several times that his hunger was never satisfied, and he blamed his plight on Mrs. Arksiatark's niggardliness. It is true that she was frugal, if I may use that mild expression; but this was only part of the explanation. Of all the women along the coast she was the least familiar with European foods. For one thing she really didn't know how to cook them. One day she would boil rice for so short a time that the grains were still hard and unswollen, and another day for so long that they burned almost to charcoal. We were all very content when she added some prunes or cheese to the pot; but some of us did not greatly relish rice that had been mixed with dried onions, or rice that was drowned in whale oil. Then there was another side to the matter, one that was even more serious. No one had ever taught her about carbohydrates and proteins and fats, or the need for a certain number of calories in the diet. Quite logically, there-fore, she equated the foreign foods with the foods with which she had always been familiar, and regarded two dry baking-powder biscuits, for example, as equivalent in food value to an equal quantity of fresh fish or fresh meat. So every one of us was half-starved, not Brick alone. And it was not at all surprising that when he and Itarklik arrived home one midnight from the fishing lake with a sledload of whitefish, we all rose from our beds and hurriedly dressed, not to extend a welcome to the wayfarers, but rather to enjoy a hearty meal of their frozen but satisfying cargo.

My housemates laughed uproariously one day when I pulled the unplucked leg of a ptarmigan out of the cooking pot and innocently put feathers and talons as well as meat into my mouth; but Mrs. Arlook did the same thing a week later. I noticed that the women gave the children the heart, the liver, and the long intestine of every ptarmigan that was shot, and that the children ate these raw. They told me, indeed, that they ate all livers raw except that of the polar bear, which they declared was poisonous; and doctors now agree with them, having recently discovered that it often causes violent nausea through an overabundance of one of the vitamins. We boiled many of the foxes that were caught in the traps, but gave our dogs all the lean ones because their flesh was too rank even for Arksiatark.

Here in the Arctic, where for more than half the year all water for either drinking or washing had to come from melted snow or ice, it would have been unreasonable to expect the standards of cleanliness one demands in more temperate climes. I realized this, and did my best to be sensible, but every now and then some action of my housemates threatened to disturb my equanimity. I could blink my eyes at the square of oilcloth which they laid on the floor for each meal, and wiped every few days with our only hand towel to erase some of the inevitable footprints. I could overlook, too, the grimy hand towel itself, which removed both perspiration and washing water from the faces of my companions, but itself never suffered the indignity of a wash. Yet I could not suppress a tinge of uneasiness whenever Mrs. Arksiatark used the same towel to wipe out my cup, and then, to insure the vessel's spotlessness, proceeded to lick away all the tea stains that clung to its rim. Rather ungraciously, too, I declined Mrs. Arlook's friendly invitation to stretch out on the bed skins and let her search my hair, a service she frequently performed for her own children and also for Brick. None of us, of course, ever indulged in a bath, or could, even had we desired one; but I myself felt airier and more comfortable without the tight-fitting woolen undershirt which many Eskimos wore beneath the loose sheep's-

fur or reindeer-fur parka, and which they seldom or never removed until it disintegrated of its own accord. It was amazing
how easily one slipped into the habit of not washing, or of washing at rare intervals only, and yet felt in no way depraved. The
physical environment itself rather encouraged the negligence; for
whereas indoors it was not possible to avoid the particles of turf
that kept seeping through the cracks in the ceiling, outdoors
there was nothing one could touch except pure white snow, and
things that were perpetually in contact with pure snow.

If it was inevitable that I should harbor suspicions about the
cleanliness of my housemates — and of myself — at no time did I
ever have reason to question their modesty. Whenever the fire in
the stove burned fiercely, and the temperature inside the cabin
climbed above 100° F., everyone except Mrs. Arlook stripped
to the waist without the slightest self-consciousness; and even she,
poor woman, did the same whenever she could unostentatiously
conceal her deformed back against a wall. But when we retired
for the night each man — and woman — skillfully pulled off his
nether garments and slid into his sleeping bag before removing
the long parka that came down nearly to his knees, although I am
quite sure that not one of them would have hesitated to expose
his or her whole person had there ever been reasonable cause,
for their actions were perfectly natural. In all the weeks that I
lodged in their cabins I did not witness a single gesture that the
most sensitive European would have branded as crude. I did
hear a few ribald stories, and am certain that the relations between the sexes were freer than our own code of conduct dictates;
but of deliberate indecency there was never a trace, despite the
lack of all privacy in their single-roomed homes.

Sewing and dressing skins kept the two women fairly busy, as
it did also the two older girls, Cookpuck and Imeroon, who
helped their mothers in many ways. Even Seeluk, Cookpuck's
younger sister, assumed charge of her baby brother for hours at
a stretch, although he was so heavy that she reeled like a drunken
sailor when she carried him around on her back. Her fur parka,
like her mother's, had been enlarged between the shoulders to

make room for the child. She would kneel down in front of him, heave him onto her back beneath the parka so that his face peered out over her shoulder, secure him with a belt tied high up on her chest, and struggle desperately to her feet. The belt and the parka then divided the strain evenly, about half of it falling on her chest and the other half on her forehead, where the outer edge of the hood made a kind of tumpline. Mrs. Arksiatark herself, being so much bigger and stronger, naturally handled the baby more efficiently. She merely dropped the front of her parka over the child's head and, swinging her body a half circle, tossed the infant high up onto her back.

The most tiresome days were the Sundays, when we generally rose late, idled about the house eating, talking, and playing cards or cat's cradles, and finally retired to bed as soon as the tedium of sitting around became no longer bearable. The women cooked, and the men sometimes cut a little firewood; but it was taboo to sew, to carpenter, even to make the round of the trap lines. The older men never dreamed of infringing this last prohibition through fear that the spirit world might take offense and cause a scarcity of game; but Brick and Jimmy, who were not only younger and more sophisticated, but also outsiders in the district without a permanent stake in its resources, slipped away once or twice to inspect their nearest traps. The women always found one time-consuming occupation that did not count as work: with a homemade bone comb, or with their fingers, they dressed and redressed their own hair and the hair of their daughters, binding the latter's with bright ribbon to keep it tidy until the following weekend.

I provided Arksiatark one Sunday with two or three sheets of paper, and asked him to sketch for me the basin of the Colville River that had been his home from boyhood. Although he had never before held a pencil in his hand he applied himself to the task with zest, and spent the greater part of the day tracing and retracing the different rivers. He and Arlook were familiar not only with the main stream, but with all its principal tributaries; they had even crossed the divide to the headwaters of another river, the Noatak, which did not flow east and then north, as did the Colville, but westward toward the setting sun. On that divide, they said, stands a mountain which the traveler should skirt as rapidly as possible; for if he lies down to rest on its slope he may never awaken again. Near the region's highest peak, Mt. Isuk, outcrops a rock (talc chlorite schist?) from which in earlier times the Eskimos carved their blubber-burning lamps; and from patches among other rocks in various localities they gathered a red earth (ocher?) which, mixed with fat, made an excellent paint. Arksiatark, who carried a pinch of this earth in his tool bag, daubed a few spots on his snow shovel, where they both registered his ownership and satisfied his craving for bright color.

Perhaps because in every community, savage as well as civilized, a man's chief critic will often be his wife, no one seemed surprised when Mrs. Arksiatark found several flaws in her husband's sketch map and undertook to draw a new one that would be more accurate. It was not just a case of feminine intuition versus masculine logic, but a genuine disagreement in interpreting the scale of the map, which was not a spatial one such as we use — not a fraction of the earth's circumference corresponding to our nautical mile, or a more or less artificial measurement of length similar to a yard or a meter — but a temporal one, based on the number of times a man would have to sleep when journeying from one place to another. This, of course, depended not only on the distance, but on the nature of the terrain (which might be smooth or rugged, flat or mountainous), on the rate at which the man marched, and on the number of hours he traveled each day. No two persons, not even husband and wife, would estimate these factors exactly alike or represent them by the same spacial intervals on a piece of paper. So Mrs. Arksiatark's map differed markedly from her husband's in the lengths of the main river sections between the mouths of the various tributaries, and in the lengths of the tributaries themselves.

There was disagreement also, but to a lesser extent, about the directions of the various streams. Lacking a magnetic compass or other means of obtaining an exact bearing, the Eskimos guided themselves by the sun and the stars, by the direction of the wind, and by readily distinguishable features in the landscape. To them a river did not flow north northwest for five miles, then curve gently eastward again for seven; instead, it flowed for about a third of a day's journey toward a far mountain or perhaps the north star, after which it curved around a hill for a short distance before resuming its earlier course. Obviously traverses as crude as this allowed abundant opportunity for widely varying interpretations on paper.

Somewhat later in the winter I encountered a different and more original method of expressing distances. An Eskimo who arrived at our cabin late one evening mentioned that he had made three halts during the day in order to boil water and brew tea. Now my journeys had taught me that it was a regular practice among the natives to halt for tea about every two and a half hours, provided the weather was clear and there was a cabin not too far ahead that offered warm shelter for the night. This man had therefore been traveling for at least eight hours; and since dogs will draw a lightly laden sled over smooth ice from dawn to dusk at an average rate of three to four miles an hour, he must have traveled approximately twenty-five miles.

Topographical details were significant to my housemates mainly in proportion to their effect on the supply of animals and fish; whence it was but natural that they should focus most of their conversation not on the mountains and rivers of the Colville basin but on its wild life. Starting from the mouth of the river, they told me, four days of hard travel during the long hours of spring brought them to a district where white men were digging for gold; and four days beyond the gold-diggers were dense forests that sheltered abundant moose. Many black bears and red foxes roamed the zone between the forests and the upper waters of the Colville, but neither species ever descended to the lower reaches of the river or overlapped the white foxes and white bears that frequented the coast. Wolverines were not uncommon within the river basin, and white sheep grazed on the slopes of many mountains, where they were rather difficult to hunt. As for cari-

The kayaker

bou, they were so numerous in earlier days that Arlook could remember a drive in which he and other Eskimos had killed more animals than they could count, the fawns alone numbering 140; yet they were only part of an enormous herd that the women and children had driven into a lake, where the hunters had overtaken them in kayaks and dispatched them with iron-tipped spears. He was but a youth at that time, but he could still recall how several deer had leaped right over his head as he crouched among the willows on the margin of the lake.

Both then and later, the Eskimos levied so heavy a toll with their spears and Winchester rifles that scores of animals had to be abandoned to the wolves and foxes, stripped only of their hides, their tongues, and the sinew along their spines. Arlook did not comprehend, apparently, that such reckless slaughter inevitably brings its own nemesis. He only knew that the great herds of caribou had mysteriously disappeared, and that most of the in-land natives, faced with starvation, had been forced to migrate to the coast. The few who still wintered near the headwaters of the Colville and other rivers were subsisting mainly on fish, although now that the number of hunters had declined so greatly the caribou were beginning to increase again.

Arlook's reminiscences touched the cords of memory of his wife, who was more familiar with a fishing line than with either rifle or spear. All the rivers and lakes teemed with whitefish, she said; and she recalled one lake which contained four or five other species as well, although the local vegetation on which their existence ultimately depended seemed no different from elsewhere except that the willows were unusually luxuriant. Far up the Colville, too, she had come upon numerous whalebones, a few of which she had raised up and set on end; and she believed that her ancestors had hunted whales from that spot during some long past era when the sea had invaded the land. Her theory seemed quite reasonable, and I might have accepted it without question had she not followed it up with the statement that wild sheep occasionally descend from the mountains and march out onto the sea ice, where they transform themselves into beluga or white whales. How had the Eskimos discovered this? Well, long ago a hunter had followed the tracks of a sheep far out on the ice until they vanished at the edge of what had clearly been open water. Furthermore, everyone knew that whenever beluga are plentiful off the coast, sheep are very scarce in the mountains; and, conversely, when sheep are plentiful in the mountains there are no beluga in the adjacent sea.

THE weather became colder as Christmas drew near, and the days so much shorter that the men often failed to make the complete circuit of their trap lines. The whistling wind blew snow through the outside entrance of our cabin down the corridor to the inner door, and even sifted a little around the edges of the door to form small white piles on the wooden floor within. Its unwarranted intrusion annoyed our two master-builders, Arlook and Arksiatark, who marched out one morning with handsaws and long knives to build a circular extension to the passage, using blocks of snow cut from a nearby drift. The blocks that formed the new walls stood firm without any support, but those of the roof rested on wooden rafters, for, as I mentioned earlier, the Alaskan Eskimos do not know how to construct a domical roof of unsupported snow. Arlook then refashioned the outside entrance, using two long rectangular snow blocks as jambs, and a third, somewhat shorter, as a lintel. Finally he set a fourth block on edge to make a kind of doorstep, to be trod, not on, but over, before descending the four steps into the circular vestibule and semi-underground passage. This doorstep was really a very clever device, because it checked the snow from drifting inward, and at the same time prevented us from sending small avalanches into the vestibule below; and the round vestibule itself was a most useful adjunct, since it gave us a storeroom in which to pile our firewood, the snow blocks that we melted for water, and a few boxes. The two men had already built a second high platform out of doors, partly to take the overflow from their first platform, and partly to hold the stores that I had brought from Cape Halkett and the sledload of fish that Brick and Jimmy freighted in a few days later from the fishing lake.

These improvements, and the addition of the second room, made our cabin quite comfortable, especially after Arlook built a sleeping bench for his family with planks that he and I sawed from driftwood. Always original, he made this bench only half the width of the room, perhaps to allow more room for his carpentry. At the same time he drove into the walls a number of wooden pegs, which took care of the clothes and other articles that had hitherto littered the floor.

If we appreciated the hard-won comfort of our humble cabin, so too did certain other living creatures; for some insects, roused from their winter sleep by what must have seemed to them an untimely warmth, emerged now and again from the turf-covered ceiling and moved sluggishly over the walls and floor. One morning I removed a tiny caterpillar that had curled up on Seeluk's face as she lay sleeping; and another day I observed a little spider descending from the ceiling by a long thread. The Eskimos viewed these half-microscopic housemates with calm indifference until a small black beetle suddenly appeared among the bed skins. Then their indifference changed to genuine alarm, because "once upon a time an individual of its species had crawled into the ear of a sleeping Eskimo and killed him."

On December 16 Jimmy set out for Barrow, taking with him Arlook's sled and a long list of supplies that he was to purchase for us at Brower's store. At noon on the day following his departure the sky put out a warning signal, beautiful but ominous. A brilliant yellow glow stretched all along the southern horizon,

Setting out for Barrow

framed above by the full leaden hue of twilight, and below by a black band of drifting snow through which the light seemed unable to penetrate. Toward the southeast the color changed to a pale green slightly tinged with red; and to the southwest the bright yellow darkened first to orange, then to a dull red that extended in a long streamer until it faded away entirely. Meanwhile the northwest breeze that had sprung up thirty-six hours before was becoming more and more gusty, and the clouds of snow rose higher and higher until they limited visibility to a few yards. Soon the stiff wind and the intense cold threatened to drive all the blood from my cheeks and forehead, and I gladly retreated to the warm shelter of our cabin.

The blizzard lasted three days, during which no one dared to wander more than a hundred yards from the house. The women occupied themselves as usual in preparing the meals and sewing, or they supervised their children's performance of the same tasks. Seated at the back of our room Cookpuck and Seeluk labored steadily at a warm mattress of loon and swan skins that was to replace the thin caribou hide on which Seeluk had been sleeping. Their mother, meantime, softened a small caribou hide with a cylindrical iron scraper, and, after cutting off a strip for Mrs. Arlook — who used it to re-sole Brick's caribou-fur boots, which had rotted with dampness — proceeded to lengthen the legs of my trousers, while I lay comfortably unclad inside my sleeping bag. Whenever we felt the urge for a little outdoor exercise we men chopped firewood. Arlook reloaded some brass shells for his shotgun, and both he and Arksiatark made new frames for drying fox skins. None of these various tasks seemed at all urgent, or created any serious disturbance. But the second morning, when Arksiatark from sheer boredom decided to prepare the breakfast himself, and cheerfully boiled together some rice, dried onions, crushed hardtack, and a little whale oil, Brick swallowed one spoonful of the unholy mixture, frantically drowned its taste with a huge mouthful of cheese, and vanished through the doorway.

The one who found the time drag most heavily was Arksiatark's grown-up son Itarklik. He brought out an old concertina, and, after droning away at a few hymns, attempted an Eskimo dance-song for which Mrs. Arlook contributed the arias. Realizing, however, that the music was only moderately successful he laid aside his instrument and began to play with a seventeen-jeweled gold watch — a more or less useless luxury in this part of the world, but stocked by Brower at his trading store because its glittering case and delicately moving parts irresistibly lured the fox skins of his unschooled but mechanically minded clients. Itarklik opened its back, stopped it, set it going again, and changed the regulator; but when the timepiece emerged from this and further tinkerings without apparent damage, he transferred his attention to another watch, one with a silver case, which obstinately refused to go even though he inserted a match into its balance to oscillate one of its wheels. He therefore took the works out and brooded over them for two days. Whether he finally made the watch go again I did not discover; but it would not have surprised me, because Eskimos are amazingly clever mechanics, whether the ob-

76

ject that needs overhauling is a watch, a rifle, a sewing machine, or a marine engine.

While we thus defied the blizzard inside the cabin, our dogs huddled out of doors in the shelter of snowbanks, from which they seldom stirred except when somebody went out to throw them a little food. One animal, however, did let curiosity get the better of discretion and begin to scramble over the roof of the house. Arksiatark yelled savagely to frighten it down, and his wife rushed to support the gut skylight lest the dog should crash through it to the floor. Then Brick and Itarklik added their shouts, and for a moment pandemonium reigned.

I suspect that the close confinement was affecting all our tempers, for Arksiatark suddenly slapped his two-year-old son and pushed him out of the way, and not long afterward the usually gentle Mrs. Arlook administered three hard slaps to her daughter Imeroon.

How dared they punish their children, I wondered, when it so obviously violated their religious code. Brick explained:

"A little baby is helpless and knows nothing; it needs protection and guidance. Hence the spirit of the dead relative or friend after whom it is named stays with it to direct its actions and protect it from all harm. But as the child grows older it learns to take care of itself, and at the age of twelve or fourteen years it can manage without the spirit, which therefore leaves it. A parent should never punish a small child because it is still under the guardianship of its namesake's spirit, which may resent the interference. But sometimes parents forget, and let themselves be carried away by their emotions."

All this seemed to me excellent psychology, even though it was expressed in the language of primitive superstition.

The blizzard ended at last, leaving across the front of our cabin a ridge of snow about 100 yards long and 6 feet or perhaps 7 feet high, down which the children gaily tobogganed on a small hand sled. In the Hudson Bay region of Canada, bush pilots of the period between the two world wars used to look down at such ridges and check their courses by them, because their axes,

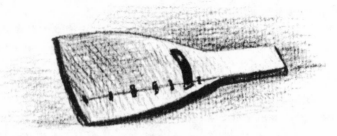

Arksiatark's snow shovel

like those of the sand dunes in the Sahara desert, run at right angles to the prevailing winds. But we humble foot-sloggers of the generation before, who traveled not by aeroplane but by dog sled, paid less attention to the ridges than we did to the shallow furrows or *sastrugi* that were scooped out by the gales; for they too were oriented at right angles to the prevailing wind, and had edges so sharp and hard that we could feel them through our skin boots.

Christmas Day, as far as the Eskimos were concerned, did not differ from other days of the year. The men left before dawn to inspect their traps, from which Arksiatark returned with three foxes, Arlook with one, and Brick, to his disappointment, empty-handed. Before they arrived home a middle-aged couple and a young boy drove up to the cabin with their sled, father and son wearing fine white coats of mountain-sheep skin. This boy had accidentally shot his younger brother seven months before, and though the tragedy seemed now forgotten, the mother's pleasant face still bore the scars of sadness.

Their visit was as welcome as it was unexpected. Mrs. Arksiatark became amazingly genial and bustled around making tea and biscuits, while Mrs. Arlook, hastily changing into her best suit and boots, engaged the guests in conversation. The trappers, when they returned, appeared just as pleased as their wives, for Arksiatark cheerfully ejaculated "ha" when he entered, and Arlook's face lit up with a silent smile. Even I came in for a little attention; for the visitor, moving suddenly over to my corner, assailed me with a heavy barrage of questions which, only half-understanding, I countered as best I could with a few stammered words.

In the Arctic more than in most places hospitality has to be governed by the state of the larder, and ours at this time could hardly have been described as well stocked. We had always lacked meat except for an occasional fox or ptarmigan; and the four foxes our trappers had just brought in, even if fat enough to be edible, were frozen solid. Outside on one of the platforms, to be sure, there were plenty of fish, but our guests had lunched on fish immediately after their arrival. For our Christmas dinner, therefore, Mrs. Arksiatark gave us boiled rice, supplemented by the inevitable biscuits and tea. There was some difficulty about dishes; but I contributed three aluminum plates, three spoons, and a frying pan, and the rest mustered another frying pan that had lost its handle, two lard-can lids, and two rectangular "tea plates" that Arksiatark resourcefully snipped from an old tobacco tin. Finally we found three more spoons, the bowl of a fourth, and two tin ladles. Armed with these motley utensils, we gathered in a ring around the rice pot and tea kettle that Mrs. Arksiatark now placed in the middle of the floor. She herself ladled out the food, measuring each individual's portion with scrupulous care; then she handed the pot to the children, and told them to clean it out with their fingers in the adjoining room. This was our Christmas dinner. The menu might perhaps have undergone some improvement, but no one could question the good cheer of the party.

A dog belonging to Arksiatark died on the following morning. It had lain ailing for several days, sheltered inside a hole in a snowbank which the children had dug and lined with shavings. Their care had been in vain, and now its owner, unable to dig a grave without immense labor — for the ground here was permanently frozen to a depth of several hundred feet, and never thawed even in midsummer except for a few inches at the surface — dragged the carcass about fifty yards from the cabin and abandoned it on top of the snow. Doubtless foxes and ravens devoured its flesh and scattered its bones over the tundra as soon as the Eskimos moved away in the spring, for that is nature's law in the Arctic. Sooner or later, indeed, Arksiatark's relatives would wrap his corpse in his bed skin or place it inside an improvised coffin of wood, and abandon it on the surface of the ground in some lonely spot, far from any inhabited dwelling, where his disembodied spirit would be unlikely to molest his surviving kin.

The Eskimos accepted the blows of fate calmly, and, when a kinsman died, sought to banish all memory of him after the first few days of mourning. Yet they were no more consistent than other peoples. Even while they strove to forget the dead man, they deliberately perpetuated his memory by conferring his name on some newborn infant, who thereby inherited the right to the same affection and attention as his namesake had enjoyed. This custom was liable to breed ill-will if the affection was not fully manifested. Brick, for example, had received two names when he was a baby, an English name from his father and an Eskimo one from his mother, who wished to commemorate the recently deceased husband of her best friend. At first the friend visited her husband's namesake quite regularly and appeared to take a deep interest in his welfare; but after a time her visits became more and more infrequent until finally they ceased altogether. This willful neglect incensed Brick's kindred, who seriously considered changing his name; in the end, however, they let the matter drop. Evidently human nature is much the same everywhere; for in our own society have not rich uncles created similar ill-will by neglecting to provide for nephews who too optimistically perpetuated their names?

On December 27 our guests drove off before dawn in order to freight back an umiak, which they had abandoned at the bottom of Harrison Bay in the previous fall, when the sea had frozen over so much earlier than anyone was anticipating. Had the skin covering of the boat been old, they would have removed it, rolled it into a bundle, and carried it away to store with their spare clothing and other goods until the spring thaw; then they would

Arlook drilling

have patched its rents, steeped it in the sea to make the seams watertight, and fastened it to the boat frame again. But the covering was new and in excellent condition, well able to withstand the winter gales. Consequently they had left it on the frame, and merely cached the boat on a hastily built platform above the high-water mark. This platform, however, stood remote from any cabin; and if the snow drifted high enough around it for a fox or a wolf to climb on top, either of those ravenous animals would make short shrift of any bearded-seal skin that was carelessly exposed to its fangs. So our visitors planned to cache their boat on one of the two platforms beside our house, where the watchful eyes of our dogs would surely protect it from all harm.

Those eyes, we discovered while they were absent, could be only too watchful. The snow had piled high around our own platforms during the recent blizzard, and some animal, almost certainly a dog, had chewed at my dog harnesses, which we had imagined to be well out of reach. I repaired one harness with strips of caribou fur, but another was damaged so badly that Mrs. Arksiatark set about making me a new one. Our unwonted activity seemed to stimulate the rest of the household; for while we were busy with the harnesses her husband began to whittle out small pump drills for his two daughters to play with, and in the adjoining room Arlook carved for his own little girl miniature figures of bears and ptarmigan.

Indoors it was warm and comfortable, but outside the weather was so cold that, when our guests returned tired and hungry, Mrs. Arksiatark prepared a special feast for them. She skinned a ptarmigan that Brick had shot during the day, boiled it with a large salted codfish left behind by Stefansson, and triumphantly served the mixed dish for the evening meal. Arlook and Arksiatark, reaching simultaneously, helped themselves to big mouthfuls of the cod; simultaneously, also, they disgorged it and dashed for the solacing blubber pot, for our cook had neglected to soak the fish before boiling it, and the strong, unfamiliar salt was more than the men could stomach. In their own diet the Eskimos did

not use salt, at least visibly, because the snow that they melted
for drinking water, and the flesh of the seals, whales, and polar
bears that formed a considerable portion of their food, contained
a high enough percentage to satisfy their physiological needs.

A desultory conversation that sprang up after supper developed
into a real council of war when Arksiatark's son Itarklik expressed his dissatisfaction with the trapping conditions around
our cabin and proposed that we divide into two groups. He
thought that his father and Arlook, who had caught a fair number of foxes, should keep their present trap lines and remain at
the cabin, with Mrs. Arlook to cook and sew for them, while he
and Brick, who had failed to catch even one fox, crossed the bay
with his mother and set their traps along its opposite shore, where
they would be nearer the whale carcasses; and he suggested that I
might accompany his party so that it could use my sled, which
was larger and stronger than his father's. If, after a reasonable
trial, the far side of the bay proved unproductive, he and Jimmy
(whom we expected back shortly from Barrow) would probably
move thirty or forty miles farther east, to try their luck in some
new district not already pre-empted by other trappers.

We shuttled the project back and forth all evening until at last
everyone agreed to it. The next morning Brick went off to gather
up his traps, while I examined my sled critically and brought
together a few things for the journey. Near me our visitor was
overhauling his sled also, for he and his family were returning
without delay to their home beyond Cape Halkett. At this period
the original Eskimo sled, with heavy runners unsurmounted by
a carriage but united by a series of stout crossbars, survived only
in a small version drawn by hand. Our visitor possessed a Euro-
pean-type sled similar to mine, with a carriage raised a foot or
more above slender runners, and with handle bars to guide the
vehicle through broken ice; but whereas my runners were shod
with steel, his carried the old-fashioned shoeing of whalebone,
which required a coating of ice before each day's journey. Such
a coating he was now putting on, not in the usual manner, by
pouring water over the runners and allowing the thin film of

Arlook's sled

liquid to freeze, but by rubbing his spittle over them, an emergency method usually reserved for the trail. It was characteristic of the experimenter Arlook that when he had overhauled his sled at the beginning of winter, he had rejected both steel shoeing and whalebone shoeing in favor of long strips of brass, which he considered to be more frictionless than steel in very cold weather. He readily admitted that brass created more friction than the thin film of ice on bone shoeing, but he objected to the latter because the film invariably wore off after a few hours' march, and the sections of whalebone were then too prone to snap their pegs and fall away, exposing the heavily dragging wood.

The visitors departed an hour and a half before daylight, when it was still so dark that the man carried a hurricane lantern to guide him along the half-obliterated trail. An hour later we too drove off, Itarklik and Brick walking ahead of the dogs to set the course. I marched on one side of the sled, little Seeluk ran behind it holding onto one of the handle bars, and her mother trudged beside her, carrying the baby boy on her back under the thick fur parka. Cookpuck, being a responsible near-adult, remained with Arksiatark. So easily did the sled glide over the hard-packed snow that we deposited Seeluk on top of it, and there the tired child fell fast asleep, wrapped in a warm caribou hide. Now and again Mrs. Arksiatark herself tried to rest by standing on the projecting ends of the sled runners, her face turned slightly to one side to shield it from the cutting breeze; but the cold soon forced her to dismount and walk briskly again to keep her blood in circulation. A light fog suffused the atmosphere, half-concealing the two youths ahead. Beyond them, invisible in the fog, lay the tiny cape for which they were steering — as nearly as they could steer their footsteps by the feel of the wind on their faces, and by the long hard furrows driven in the snow by the prevailing east and west gales. For the wind and the sastrugi are the compasses of the Eskimo, whenever there are no landmarks to guide him and the sun and stars are hidden.

Mrs. Arksiatark's stamina was amazing. No sooner had we reached the opposite shore and halted our sled beside a large log of driftwood than she sent Itarklik away to search for more wood, told Brick to feed the dogs with whale blubber, and herself, unaided, set about erecting a tent, burdened though she was with the two-year-old baby on her back. First she planted in the snow a circle of willow sticks that we had brought on the sled, arched over and lashed together their tips, and roofed the dome-shaped framework with our canvas sled cover. Then she piled loose snow around the edges of the canvas to keep out the drafts, laid a few sticks across the floor on which to spread the bedding, and carried inside the food and cooking utensils. I meanwhile had chopped some firewood and set up the stove, so that it was not long before we were dining on frozen fish, steaming rice, and hot tea.

The makeshift tent was cold and comfortless throughout the night, even though it shielded us from the sweep of the northeast wind. A thick layer of frost rimmed the mouth of my sleeping bag where the low temperature congealed my breath, and my feet at the bottom of the bag felt like two blocks of solid ice. Inevitably I rose early, and, after lighting the stove, crept quietly out of doors to collect more firewood, hoping not to disturb my roommates; but Mrs. Arksiatark, who also was awake, having passed an equally uncomfortable night, bestirred herself immediately to bake a few biscuits for our breakfast. These biscuits, half

Mrs. Arksiatark's tent

a frozen fish apiece, and some strong tea fortified us for the strenuous task that lay ahead of us. With the first glimmer of dawn everyone turned out to build a log cabin.

Again the indomitable Mrs. Arksiatark took over the leadership, though she must still have been tired from her exertions of the day before. She was both architect and master-builder, knowing far more about camp life and the construction of a log cabin than the rest of us combined. With a small axe, an adze, and a shovel — our only tools — we split some driftwood logs into rough planks and erected the frame of a house approximately 11 feet by 8 feet at the base and 5 feet high, with a roof that was virtually flat and walls that sloped gently inward to support more readily their banking of turf. On the south side facing the light we made a small doorway, over which we suspended our sled cover; and we banked the roof as well as the walls with turf and soft snow. Darkness set in long before we finished the insulation of the roof; and it was a very tired and famished party that sat down at last for another frozen-fish meal.

Even then we were not altogether happy. The cabin was indeed larger and warmer than the tent of the night before, but its roof trickled water on our heads from the moment we lit the stove. We had expected a number of leaks as soon as the warmth within melted the snow that clung to the ceiling logs and the ice that was imbedded in the frozen turf of the roof; for no new dwelling of

this type, however carefully constructed, can escape a preliminary
baptism, especially if it has been built in the depth of winter. But
the drips should never have become a cascade, and they should
have ceased entirely after a few hours when all the turf had dried
out. Owing to the dearth of driftwood, however, and to the short-
ness of the daylight, we had left wide spaces between the rafters of
the roof, and accepted a turf insulation so thin that the warmth
penetrated right through it to the covering of snow on the outside. In consequence, we dined, one might say, in the rain. Fortunately the dripping stopped as soon as the fire died down, and
we passed a very comfortable night.

NEW YEAR'S Day, 1914. My
diary describes the setting thus:

"I am living in a tiny one-roomed house of driftwood, turf
and snow that I myself helped to construct, with an elderly lady
of perhaps 35–40 years and her two children, a girl of about 8 and
a boy of 2 years. For food we have a little rice which we boil,
frozen fish which we eat raw, I skinning and slicing it with my
sheath-knife, the other two with their curiously-shaped ulos. Tea
and sugar supplement this diet, while the two or three biscuits
are reserved for the children. We have a stove to burn wood, a
primus stove and a very little coal-oil (or kerosene), skins and
sleeping clothes, 3 or 4 pots, a kettle and a frying pan, with a
couple of plates, 3 spoons and 4 cups. A string across the ceiling
near the stove enables us to hang up our boots, mitts, etc. to dry.
For light we have 4 candles besides the one which is now burning: Itarklik and Brick have taken the lantern. For clothes I have
an inner and an outer deerskin shirt (the latter I seldom need)
with a snow shirt of blue denim to wear on top, a pair of deerskin
mitts made for me by Mrs. Arksiatark (they are bad, for the fur
is coming out; the skin from which they were made was very
poor), a pair of deerskin trousers with burberry knee-breeks over

them, an inner and an outer pair of deerskin boots. The boots are badly made and very cumbersome, so when the weather is not very cold and I am not likely to be standing about in the snow, I wear two pairs of woolen socks, a pair of sheepskin socks and light deerskin boots over them. Then there is my sleeping bag, also of deerskin; its fur too comes out much more than it should. My home is for the time being on the west side of a large bay which forms the western portion of Harrison Bay—about 100 miles east of Point Barrow. The temperature is apparently the ordinary mid-winter temperature here; what it is in degrees I do not know, having no thermometer, but it must be uniformly considerably below zero. The sun has been invisible for 6 weeks, and the twilight lasts about 5 hours."

The morning after we built the cabin Itarklik and Brick drove off to the little settlement near Cape Halkett to bring back flour, whale blubber, and any other supplies they could procure for ourselves and our dogs; and as soon as they departed Mrs. Arksiatark wandered south along the coast to set a few fox traps, leaving Seeluk at home to look after her baby brother. The little girl discharged her responsibility most faithfully; whether she played with the child inside the house on the bed skins, or outside in the snow, she never abandoned it for a single moment. I meanwhile returfed those places on the roof of the cabin that had dripped too freely the night before, and then set about building a short corridor that would prevent the wind from whistling into the house around the edges of the cloth-covered door. Not being as skillful as the Eskimos in handling large blocks of snow I did not finish the second task until the following afternoon. In fact, I was still working on it when Mrs. Arksiatark returned from a visit to her trap line. That Arctic veteran surveyed my handiwork with a Mona Lisa smile and murmured as she passed on, "You have built it very well"—a falsehood so palpable, and so unexpected, that it left me quite speechless.

Our foragers returned with four sacks of flour, two cupfuls of rice (a present from our friends near Cape Halkett), and a formidable supply of whale blubber, some of it still adhering to the

Mrs. Arksiatark

mammal's thick black skin. We welcomed them gladly, for even Mrs. Arksiatark admitted that we had been half-starved during the previous three days. To celebrate the occasion, she immediately boiled half the rice and baked an extra quantity of biscuits; and we rounded off a hearty meal with morsels of the black whale skin, a popular food that probably contains a certain amount of nourishment, even though it tastes like licorice and has the consistency and springiness of pure rubber.

We could now count on abundant food to last us two weeks. However, Mrs. Arksiatark, with her usual foresight, determined that it should last at least three, and held us down to two biscuits apiece for breakfast, and one frozen fish and one biscuit for supper. To be sure, little Seeluk and her baby brother were never hungry, because as children they had the privilege of helping themselves to any food that lay within their reach, and they exercised their privilege all day long. Mrs. Arksiatark too was quite content, having known little except hunger all her life. But the rest of us were not happy, not even Itarklik; and one evening, after his mother had crept into her sleeping bag, he brought forth a lump of blubber half the size of a round cheese, which he and Brick consumed to the last morsel. I could have shared their banquet — indeed, they cordially invited me to do so; but I preferred to fast, remembering that only four days before I had tried to get rid of my hunger with a quite moderate portion of black-skin and blubber, and the blubber had nearly got rid of me.

Itarklik and Brick now devoted all their attention to trapping, and the former staked his claims along the shore north of our cabin, while Brick took possession of the shore to the south and southeast, beginning from the spot, about a mile distant, where Mrs. Arksiatark had planted her last trap. Fortune smiled on both of them, for within three days Brick had caught one fox — his first — and Itarklik two. The latter, after skinning each of his victims, cut its throat at the first vertebra until its head dangled by a mere shred of flesh. He was releasing, he said, the animal's spirit, which would quickly reincarnate itself and thus help to maintain the fox population. Whether later he cut also a tiny sliver from its fur before selling it I do not know, but many of the older Eskimos did so, not from fox furs only, but from all pelts, lest the spirits of the dead animals should be tempted to follow their coats to some distant land. It was to the neglect of this custom, and not to excessive slaughter with firearms — the true cause — that they attributed the scarcity of caribou in their region; and some of them feared that the polar bears also would decrease in number now that several hunters, violating another ancient custom, were removing the skin from that animal's claws and head.

While my companions were patrolling their trap lines I cut the firewood for them and kept a pot of melted snow on the stove so that they could slake their thirst as soon as they returned to camp. They wondered sometimes why I too did not lay down a trap line, since rifles and ammunition, flour, sugar, and many other things that had now become necessities to them appeared unobtainable except by furs. When the Canadian government organized our expedition, however, it expressly forbade us to interfere in the fur trade, or to trap any of the fur-bearing animals, unless we needed them for food, for clothing, or for scientific specimens. Even without this prohibition I doubt whether I could have found the heart to set any fox traps after witnessing the torture they inflicted on the unhappy creatures. The steel jaws nearly always closed around one foreleg, holding the struggling victim prisoner until death released it from its pain. One of Arlook's foxes fought so hard to free itself that it tore away the skin from its ankle almost to the hip. I discovered it frozen to death, its second leg drawn up close to the body and its lips parted in an agonized snarl. Probably in its day this fox had torn to pieces many a gentle ptarmigan, and gobbled up more than one harmless marmot, but does man need to emulate nature's cruelty when his own life is not at stake?

Although in theory a trapper should inspect his trap line daily, in practice this was neither necessary nor indeed possible, since blizzards sometimes confined everyone indoors for two or three days at a stretch, and, besides, the majority of the Eskimos observed the missionary ban on Sunday labor. It really made very

Eskimo dog

little difference whether a fox remained five hours in a trap or fifty, because its pelt could suffer no harm in temperatures that ranged persistently far below the freezing point. I felt no hesitation, therefore, in asking Brick to desert his trap line for a day or two and join me in freighting half our stock of flour across the bay to Arksiatark and his housemates, who were contending with a diet just as restricted as our own.

Actually it was more restricted than we had imagined, for, unaware that we had left some rice on one of the platforms, they were living on fish and blubber alone. Not that this was any great hardship for them. Their forefathers had lacked all vegetable food except a few berries and an occasional root; and they themselves were quite accustomed to eat nothing but caribou meat, or fish, for several weeks at a time, especially during the summer months when they were hunting inland. But now Arksiatark was sick. Angry rashes spotted his upper body and arms, and his chest was racked by a hacking cough and by a pain in the region of his right lung. When Brick and I arrived at his cabin he was sitting, stripped to the waist, beside the stove, baking his chest and back alternately. Although I suspected that he had contracted pleurisy,

I could not prescribe a remedy, for I neither was sure of my diagnosis nor possessed any medicines. Mrs. Arlook, however, with her inherited fear of witchcraft and the enmity of supernatural spirits, was quite sure that some malevolent person had bewitched her brother's food, or that he himself had unconsciously broken some taboo. As soon as we arrived, therefore, she cut off his fish-and-blubber diet for a day and fed him nothing but biscuits made from the flour we had brought them, on the assumption that no sorcerer could possibly contaminate this non-Eskimo food. Yet even the change of diet failed to bring him any relief; and after being tormented most of the night by the ceaseless irritation of his body, he kindled a hot fire in the stove and huddled beside it until daylight.

There could be no doubt that his illness was creating considerable anxiety; and yet there was a restfulness in the home, a lack of strain that had never been evident before, indicating that all the tension had stemmed from Mrs. Arksiatark and vanished with her departure. Even Cookpuck was visibly brighter and less inhibited. Her father was invariably kind to her, and now that her mother was absent, her aunt and uncle, in whose room she generally slept under the same fur robe as her cousin Imeroon, openly showed her the same affection as they bestowed on their own daughter. So she was unusually cheerful that evening as, sitting beside her aunt, she sewed up some rents in my sleeping bag, while Mrs. Arlook herself reshaped my ungainly fur boots and her husband labored over a pair of snowshoes.

It was late the following afternoon when Brick and I regained the trapping cabin, but the news of her husband's illness so disturbed Mrs. Arksiatark that she would have started out immediately and crossed the bay in the darkness had we not persuaded her to delay a day and take up her fox traps. This she did the next morning, and before noon she and I hitched up the dogs and drove off, leaving Itarklik and Brick, whose traps were more remote, to follow at their leisure.

We arrived at our destination while it was still light, the distance being probably not more than twelve miles. Only Arlook came outside to greet us; of Arksiatark there was no sign. I expected his wife to hurry indoors without delay, but she merely asked Arlook how her husband was, and then lingered, quite needlessly, to help me unhitch the dogs and unload the sled. Yet I think her apparent unconcern was merely a pose, because when I entered the cabin some minutes later she was sitting at Arksiatark's side, displaying all the solicitude one would expect from a genuinely devoted wife. The invalid himself had improved considerably: although his voice was still weak, the pain in his chest had vanished, the rashes were less troublesome, and his appetite was excellent. While he hesitated as yet to go outdoors he felt active enough to carve for his baby boy a wooden gun modeled on a two-foot weapon that Arlook had made for his daughter Imeroon some days before.

It was not easy for hunters as energetic as these two men to limit their outdoor activities to five or six hours of winter twilight, and then to mope inside the cabin for the remaining eighteen hours of the day. They chopped firewood and skinned their foxes, carved toys for their children, and made the necessary household tools and utensils. Yet time still hung heavy on their hands, and their exceptional ingenuity and mechanical skill found little or no outlet. It weighed just as heavily on the women, who seldom went outside the house, but cooked and sewed, and sewed and cooked, from morning until bedtime.

One afternoon I watched Mrs. Arlook making a pair of boots for her daughter Imeroon. She possessed neither yardstick nor measuring tape, lacked even a pattern except the image in her brain; but she knew that the length of the child's boot sole should be the span of one hand plus the breadth of two fingers, and with this measure in her mind she cut out the caribou hide without a falter. In doing so she held her small crescentic knife at a 45° angle, thereby beveling the pieces of skin so that they fitted together more closely, something she could not have done with a pair of scissors. Meat she cut with a similar but larger knife, the *ulo,* which for many purposes was more efficient than her husband's hunting knife; by rocking it back and forth, leaning her whole weight on it, she could slice right through a slab of solidly frozen meat or fish that Arlook's knife would hardly nick.

Her boot-making progressed by fits and starts as she laid the pieces of fur aside, and took them up again, whenever the spirit moved her. At supper time she put them away altogether and gossiped idly with the rest of us; but a little later, when I was writing some Eskimo expressions in my notebook, she interrupted me, saying:

"Jennessi" (so they vocalized my name) "let's race each other at cat's cradles."

Nothing loath, I pulled out the loop of string I invariably carried with me and plied my fingers as rapidly as I could whenever she called the tune. Arksiatark watched us indulgently, and at a pause in the game remarked:

"You know, there is a 'spirit of cat's cradles' which some of our shamans can control. I have seen a shaman extend an imaginary loop of string, and hold suspended in mid-air three fur belts that were laid across it. Once, too, when I was a small boy playing alone in the house with my mother, we heard a loud crackling sound as if some dried skins were shaking in the wind. My mother raced outdoors, circled the house as fast as she could, and re-entering, sat down again to listen; but the crackling did not recur. It came, she said, from the 'spirit of cat's cradles.' "

Arlook, who had listened to his brother-in-law as attentively as the rest of us, now related his own experience on the Noatak River, where he had spent the greater part of his boyhood.

"Once the Noatak Eskimos built a dance house in anticipation of a festival, and practiced their dances inside it before sending messengers to invite their neighbors. Another boy and I went out to bring more food, and while we were absent some of the children, disregarding the warnings of their elders, made a loud uproar. Everything seemed normal when I returned, but a few minutes later we heard a sharp report outdoors and a crackling as of dried skins. The noise traveled around the house until it reached the door, which was merely an opening covered by a curtain of skin. Through this opening poured a stream of mist, and, concealed by the mist, the spirit of cat's cradles. The lamps at first flared brightly, but slowly they dimmed and began to expire, one after the other, while we sat paralyzed with fear. Darker and darker became the house. From time to time some old man cried 'Will no one go outside?' But no one stirred.

"My grandfather, who was sitting on one of the benches, called to me, and when I ran to him quickly, he lifted me onto his knee. Fearfully we waited. At last an old man snatched up a lamp that still remained lit, and, racing through the mist, carried it outdoors and around the house. The spirit of cat's cradles vanished immediately; and although the wind extinguished the old man's lamp, the people were able to relight it, and then relight all the other lamps. Presently, however, the old man's hands became very cold, and he sat motionless and silent, unable to move or even to answer when his brother asked him what was the matter. Some shamans exerted their magic power upon him, and by morning he could walk again; but his speech did not return until some days later. Had he not carried one of the lamps outside before they all expired every person in the dance house would have become paralyzed and died."

On January 15 the sun, which had been invisible since November 20, gave every promise of rising over the horizon, but at the last moment deferred its appearance until the next day. As the light was beginning to fade again Itarklik sighted a sled approaching from the direction of the fishing lake and warned us that Kunarluark was at hand with his wife and son.

An outsider might have thought the reception we gave them intentionally cool; for, apart from myself, the only persons who were visible when they drew up in front of the cabin were Itarklik and the children, and Itarklik, who was cleaning a fox fur, continued to stamp it in the snow as if he were totally unaware of their presence. Not until they were unharnessing their dogs did the Arlooks and Mrs. Arksiatark emerge and shake hands; and even they stood aside and looked on in silence as Brick came forward, shook hands also, and casually turned away to cut up some firewood. No one offered to help with either dogs or sled, perhaps because no help was needed. Yet our visitors entered the cabin without any hesitation, hung up their boots and mittens wherever they could find room for them, and seemed to feel completely at home. Mrs. Kunarluark, a generous, warmhearted chatterbox, even complained that the cabin was too warm, and, pulling off her fur parka, bustled about the room, half-naked, while she presented each of us with a hard ship's biscuit smeared with a thick layer of canned butter that she had brought in from her sled. Then she handed Mrs. Arksiatark a tin of condensed milk for her baby, and would have suckled the child had it not torn itself petulantly from her arms. Half an hour later she undertook to prepare our supper, and, mixing a small canful of meat with some macaroni, set it on the stove to boil; but as she moved back and forth in the unfamiliar room she kicked over a tin of blubber that had been carelessly abandoned close to the door. "Arrah," she cried in dismay, stepping backward when the greasy oil began to spread relentlessly farther and farther over the floor. But little Cookpuck was equal to the emergency: she quickly snatched up a bag of feathers, and, spilling out part of the contents, wiped up the mess before it could cause any damage.

The bountiful and, to me, appetizing supper that our guest prepared for us that evening made me more dissatisfied than ever with the semistarvation diet I had been enduring since mid-December. We had practically exhausted the food that Stefansson had left me; and the supplies he had promised to send around Christmas from our expedition's base in Camden Bay had failed to arrive, although it was now mid-January. Each day I scanned the eastern sky in the hope of sighting a sled, but in vain. Yet one would surely come, I thought, before the month ended; and I could hold out for two more weeks if I could purchase some supplies from Brower's brother-in-law Assuark, who, after a quick trip to Barrow, had taken over Kunarluark's cabin near Cape Halkett while the latter and his family occupied their tent at the fishing lake. Accordingly, I hitched up my dogs, and, accompanied by Brick, drove off across Harrison Bay.

We reached our destination without mishap and put up, as be-

En route

fore, at Angopcana's cabin; but hardly had we carried our sleeping bags inside his dwelling than we received an invitation to dine with his neighbor Assuark. Both these families were plutocrats compared with the spartan household of Arksiatark. Day and night alike their cabins were brightly lit with two and sometimes three lamps, and at evening their tables positively groaned — or, more correctly, their floors creaked — with the abundance of both Eskimo and European food. The ubiquitous baking-powder biscuits appeared at every meal, to be sure, but always with butter, and only to supplement some more substantial dish such as meat, either canned or frozen, potatoes, or lima beans. Foods like rice and cornmeal they seasoned with salt instead of by burning, flavored with sugar and canned milk, and ate from European dishes of which they possessed an ample supply. At night, to make me more comfortable, my hostesss supplied me with two cushions, luxuries that Mrs. Arksiatark would hardly have tolerated in her home. That lady would have appreciated more highly the abundant tobacco, perhaps also the inexhaustible chewing gum, that ultra-modern luxury-necessity which she and her family were just beginning to discover. Here among the trappers nearer Barrow gum was as popular as among baseball communities in countries farther south. Yet a politically minded traveler might have noticed an important difference, for whereas the baseball capitalist insists on unrestricted private ownership of his

stick of gum, the communistic Eskimo, more enlightened, willing-
ly shared his stick with other members of his local unit. Being a
conscientious Marxist, he masticated his fair share only, then
pasted the residue to the ceiling of the cabin, or to one of its posts,
where it would be accessible to the jaws of his proletarian com-
rades.

These Halkett families were not inlanders, but coastal natives
who had seen ships come and go each summer for nearly half a
century. Naturally, they were more sophisticated than the house-
holds of Arksiatark and Arlook. They disliked Mrs. Arksiatark
intensely, and retailed some very unpleasant stories about her
treatment of Cookpuck. On one occasion, they said, blind Mrs.
Angopcana had offered to adopt the girl to protect her from
further ill-usage, but the father had withheld his consent. Of
Arlook they spoke with respect, but their gossip left me with a
distinct impression that they looked upon him and all inland
Eskimos as poor country cousins — fine caribou hunters, no doubt,
but deserving of pity, because they were lacking in worldly
knowledge and deprived of the many advantages that enriched
the lives of their more forunate kindred on the coast.

My artist friend Two Wolves, who had entertained us so
pleasantly on my last visit to Halkett, had now moved to another neighborhood, perhaps because he had exhausted his
repertoire of folk tales and needed a new audience. His wife had
died childless many months before, leaving him a widower with
no responsibilities, but at the same time without his own woman
to cook for him and to make and mend his clothing. He therefore drifted from house to house, hunting and trapping like
other men to pay for his board and lodging, and performing for
the housewife various odd jobs, such as chopping wood and carrying snow, in return for her care of his wardrobe. Sooner or later
he was sure to marry again; but in the meantime, being strong
and active, he was an asset rather than a liability and so was
welcomed everywhere. Young children left in similar circumstances sometimes fared less happily, judging from the numerous
folk tales that described how orphans had been grievously abused

by their foster-parents but had avenged themselves in later years through the help of supernatural spirits.

I myself, being neither a trapper nor a successful hunter, would have constituted a grave liability to any household had I not commanded unlimited credit on Brower's store at Barrow. It was for this reason that Assuark did not hesitate to turn over to me the small quantity of supplies that he could spare, accepting as payment my note for double their quantity; and Mrs. Angopcana's melancholy voice — so characteristc of blind people — carried a note of real warmth as she invited me to move into her home if life became too unpleasant on the other side of Harrison Bay. Doubtless it comforted them to know that their kindnesses would meet with fitting recompense. Nevertheless, I was deeply grateful when Assuark filled my hurricane lantern in the darkness of the early morning and came outside to help us load our sled, and no less grateful when Mrs. Angopcana sent out to us, as her parting gift, ten pounds of nutritious beans; for these were spontaneous actions not tainted by any hope of reward. Most Eskimos are by nature very generous, and Angopcana's household in particular was known along the whole coast for its hospitality to all travelers, native and white alike.

NOTHING unusual had occurred at our Harrison Bay home during our brief absence. When Brick and I walked in, soon after dark, Arksiatark was sitting in the far corner of his room diligently working down a file into a hunting knife. His cough continued to trouble him a little, and he still confined himself rather closely to the house, but otherwise he seemed quite recovered. Mrs. Arksiatark was scraping a caribou hide in front of the stove; and against the rear wall Seeluk was playing with her baby brother. Lanky Itarklik lay drowsing on his back in the near corner of the room, having just returned from inspecting his father's trap line; Brick, worn out from the day's journey, immediately flung himself down beside him and fell fast asleep. In the adjoining room Arlook was shaping a pair of willow snowshoes, using for tools his hunting knife, an old-fashioned bow drill, and a small frame saw made from a clock spring. His wife sat beside him, twisting sinew for the lashings of the snowshoes; and under the sleeping bench Cookpuck and her cousin Imeroon were sewing.

So hot was the cabin that everyone except Mrs. Arlook had

stripped to the waist; their bodies, a creamy white in daylight but reddish in the lamp glow, cast blurred shadows on the dark walls around. A hurricane lantern hung on the front wall of each room, but remained unlit through lack of kerosene. The only illumination came from two blubber-burning lamps made from empty tobacco cans, whose lids were slotted for calico wicks; the wick of Arlook's lamp could be raised or lowered by means of a wooden pin. Even for these lamps fuel was in short supply, although during the autumn Arksiatark had cached two hundred pounds of blubber at Cape Halkett inside a sealskin poke. I would have rolled this poke onto my sled and brought it back with me had I possessed more than four dogs, or a sled less heavily laden. As it was, Mrs. Arksiatark, accompanied by Brick, made a special trip for it some days later.

On January 23 Jimmy arrived from Barrow with an almost empty sled, having cached most of its load near Cape Halkett on one of Angopcana's platforms. He brought me a very small quantity of provisions, and a large packet of letters all written at least six months before. To Arksiatark he gave a new pack of playing cards, much to the delight of that old hunter, who had pined for a game of "patience" during the long hours of his convalescence. Patience was the only card game with which he and his wife were familiar; but at Barrow the natives greatly preferred a derivative of poker introduced, apparently, by the Lap herdsmen who brought the first domesticated reindeer to Alaska in the final quarter of the nineteenth century.

During the preceding weeks Mrs. Arlook had been humming a tune so melodious that I transcribed it in my notebook. I now discovered that she had learned it from Jimmy, who had himself composed it when he was imprisoned in the ice on board the *Karluk* and despaired of seeing again his home at Point Hope. After we left the *Karluk* and made our way to Barrow he taught the song to several families along the coast. They too found it melodious; its popularity grew with each new audience and it soon became the latest "hit," a position that it maintained all winter. When Mrs. Arlook told Jimmy that I too liked his song

Jimmy

Jimmy's song

he gave me a private rendition, lying back among the bed skins and beating time with a stick. I noticed at once that his version — the original one, of course — differed slightly from Mrs. Arlook's, and that both differed from other versions I had heard before, and was to hear again this winter; whence I concluded that the Eskimos are as prone to modify or corrupt their songs as we are. Later I sent a copy of this melody to an organist in England, who harmonized it and played it several times in his church as a voluntary. There also it met with approbation, for several members of the congregation asked him the name of its composer.

One, who knew it already, graciously thanked him for his "lovely selection from Bach."

It seemed to me that Arksiatark and his wife resented the presence of Jimmy in their home, although he rarely lingered in their room but slept and spent most of his time in Arlook's. To be sure he was an outsider, more traveled and more sophisticated than they were: a man of the world who knew all the latest card tricks and all the latest gossip. But there may have been another reason — professional jealousy; for Arksiatark himself cherished ambitions in the world of song. Earlier in the winter one of his compositions had been the vogue, not only in our household, but at Cape Halkett; and it might still have been popular had not Jimmy suddenly appeared out of nowhere and eclipsed it with his own melody. Be that as it may, Arksiatark and his wife remained strangely silent in their room whenever Jimmy and the others broke forth in song; and the cloud which had been hovering over the household for several weeks appeared a little darker.

One evening Mrs. Arlook, weary of continuous sewing, took refuge in a game of patience. When that palled, she lay back on the bed and, in a loud, rather nasal voice, chanted those meaningless syllables, *ai yanga ye ai yanga ye ye yai,* that form the burden of every Eskimo song, and sometimes the text also. She ended each verse with another characteristic feature of Eskimo music — a loud emission of breath rather like a sigh. The song, though wordless, appeared to be well known, because her husband had no difficulty in maintaining perfect accord with her, despite the frequent changes of time. So successful was the entertainment that Jimmy, Brick, and Itarklik joined them the next evening and expanded the duet into a full choir. Jimmy appointed himself conductor; he improvised new words to old tunes, and even invented one or two new ones which he then taught to his companions. The house echoed and re-echoed as their melodies rose and fell, and Mrs. Arlook's shrill treble drowned out the male voices whenever the chorus tended to die down. Some of the songs were constructed in verses separated by a refrain; but whereas the verses carried a few significant words, the refrains

contained only meaningless syllables. Even the words were prosaic
and commonplace, for Jimmy unhappily lacked the true Pindaric
fire. Yet he struck a startling note in one improvisation by in-
troducing into the refrain five English words which he had picked
up somewhere without understanding their meaning:

VERSE

e ye yai yanga e yai
teriganiaruk tautukiga tatpiga
sikuliami kimaktuarkara

("A fox I saw it up there: on the young ice it was fleeing")

REFRAIN

e ye yai yanga
Father Son and Holy Ghost
e ye yanga yai

Like her parents, Cookpuck remained aloof from all these con-
certs, but for a very different reason. She spent most of her time
in a corner of Arlook's room under the sleeping platform, or
else against the back wall of her parents' quarters where she
would attract little or no attention. Though she spoke very rarely,
except perhaps to Imeroon, nothing happened without her
noticing it. Did some one begin to narrate a story? There she
was listening with both ears. Did Arlook show me a new cat's-
cradle figure? She watched and learned it too. Her mother scolded
her quite often, and even Mrs. Arlook reproved her on one or
two occasions; yet at no time did I see her display either annoy-
ance or sulkiness. Her obedience was exemplary: she might have
been Griselda. When playing with the other children, happy
and apparently carefree, she seemed more like their governess
than their playmate, so quiet was she, so grave and so watchful.
Life had buffeted and matured her beyond her years: She had
the responsible air of a married woman, although she was still
only twelve and not likely to marry for at least two years.

Those two years she would number by seasons, not by days or
even months; for a monotonous timelessness had invaded us
during this long midwinter period, a feeling that the world was
standing still. Both Arlook and Itarklik—probably also Arksia-

tark — possessed watches, but they regarded them as playthings rather than as measures of time's passing or regulators of the daily activities. Our only regulators were the never-failing ones that nature provided, daybreak and the approach of night. Each individual rose at his own time in the morning, yet always before dawn because the daylight was so short. The men left immediately for their trap lines, rarely waiting for breakfast unless the kettle was already boiling; but the rest of us frequently lingered in bed until Mrs. Arksiatark placed biscuits and tea kettle in the middle of the floor and summoned us to eat. The main meal was invariably timed for the onset of darkness; and we retired whenever we became too weary, or too bored, to stay up any longer. As soon as one person began to undress the others usually did likewise, removing the lower garments first, then sliding into the sleeping bag and throwing off the long parka. The little children were no more bound to a definite bedtime hour than their parents: they just lay down and slept whenever and wherever they felt inclined. At times one of the little girls would stretch herself out on the floor between the two rooms, her head and body in one and her legs in the other so that no one could pass without stepping over her; yet only later, when we ourselves were preparing for bed, would the mother drag her to her usual sleeping place. Cookpuck alone, the family Cinderella, generally stayed up until her mother had settled down in bed for the night, for fear that she might be called upon to bring in blubber or to perform some other task.

A young man, Kunarluark's son, dropped in one afternoon from the fishing lake. What prompted his visit I do not know, but he was evidently Arksiatark's guest rather than Arlook's, since he played cards with Mrs. Arksiatark most of the evening and slept in their room alongside me. Moreover, his visit provoked Mrs. Arksiatark to unusual lavishness, for she cooked and set in front of us twice the usual number of biscuits. Thereupon Mrs. Arlook, not to be outdone, suddenly produced from her room an even larger number, baked so much better that even Arksiatark dipped from her bowl first, and only reached for his wife's biscuits after his sister's had disappeared.

The bountifulness of this meal in no way affected our table manners. We gathered as usual in a ring, six men and two women; and, for the benefit of our visitor, Mrs. Arksiatark delivered a short grace, always omitted when we ate alone. Hardly had she uttered the last syllable when eight jaws began to work convulsively. Now and then a diner fingered two or three biscuits before making his choice; but time was short, and the laggard was likely to go hungry. Between mouthfuls of biscuits we gulped down cupfuls of tea; for the two kettles, despite their cargo of leaves, held enough liquid to fill each person's cup two and even three times. "Hurry" was our dinner motto. "Your own brother will empty the teapot and eat most of the biscuits unless you get there before him." Yet everyone was cheerful and good-humored. Whatever happened, the children would not suffer, because their mothers had set ample portions aside for them, to be eaten in the background; and I, who was certainly not the fittest in this struggle for survival, was assured of safety by Mrs. Arksiatark, who had reserved two biscuits under the stove for my consumption later.

The days were becoming perceptibly longer, and when the air was still we could feel a soft warmth in the rays of the midday sun. Arlook greatly brightened his room by setting a rectangular block of snow on edge behind his skylight, where it reflected the sun's rays inward; and Arksiatark promptly followed his example. In spite of the increasing daylight, however, the temperature remained as low as before, except when a brief spell of mild weather presaged an approaching gale. One gale sent us a more visible warning: it provoked the sun into "steadying itself with two walking sticks lest it should be driven from its course by the oncoming storm." At least that was how the Eskimos explained the strange phenomenon. Less imaginative scientists would have dismissed it as two parhelia or mock suns, one on each side of the real sun, created by peculiar conditions in the atmosphere.

February 1 arrived, and still there was no sign of a sled from the east bringing me the promised supplies. Our food was running low again, and our dogs were on short rations. The hungry animals continually prowled around the camp searching for something to eat. One night two clambered onto the cabin roof. We shouted and shouted, but in vain. Someone had to turn out in the darkness to drive them down, and the logical person seemed to be me, because I was sleeping nearest the door. Pulling on my trousers and socks, therefore, I groped down the black corridor to the open air; but the miscreants had vanished into the night before I reached the entrance, and my only reward was a shower of snow on my naked back as my head struck the corridor roof.

More tragic at this time was the loss of one of my dogs. Apparently it had dislocated its jaw in a fight, for it was unable to close its mouth and began to act very strangely. Twenty-four hours later its jaw was still wide open and its tongue frozen white. The tortured animal howled so piteously whenever we or another dog approached that I ended its agony with a bullet, then dragged its body onto the ice in order that the sea might carry it away at the beginning of summer.

This left me with only three dogs for the trip to Barrow which I dared no longer postpone. However, Brick owned two, one that he had brought with him and another that his mother had sent with Jimmy. While he was taking up the three fox traps that he had set in this part of Harrison Bay, I overhauled our harnesses; then, leaving on Arksiatark's platform our tent and stove, which we were not likely to need on the journey, we gathered together the remainder of our possessions in readiness for the morning.

Long before dawn we rose, loaded the sled, and began to harness the dogs. Two were missing, and with so many tracks all around it was impossible to tell which way they had gone, and whether together or separately. Brick hurried off in one direction, I in another. Half an hour later I sighted one of the animals wandering aimlessly along the shore. The other Brick discovered in a fox trap, so crippled that it could only hobble on three legs. It had been the most intelligent dog in my team, capable of leading the

A blizzard

others and of following a trail without guidance. Now, with its leg frozen and probably broken, it was useless. Hoping that it might recover after a few weeks, I asked Arksiatark to take care of it until my return; but he demurred, saying that he was too short of food, and I dared not make the same request of Arlook through fear of stirring up discord. About noon, therefore, Brick and I started out to cross Harrison Bay with the unharnessed dog limping beside the sled. Very soon it tired and lay down to rest, whimpering. I lifted it up and placed it on top of our sleeping bags where it would be warm and comfortable; but every time the sled lurched the poor beast took fright and jumped down. This continued until it was impossible to carry it any farther. Then, very reluctantly, I shot it, rather than abandon it to perish from starvation and cold, or to be destroyed by a wolf.

By mid-afternoon the sun had set and darkness was closing in. We had been following the well-marked trail to "Igloo 2," the trapping cabin that we had built in the southwest corner of the bay; but now a new and formidable crack in the ice barred our way. Actually it was less than three feet wide and frozen over; but the dogs refused to go near it, wisely perhaps, because the old ice along its edges may have been treacherous and the new ice in between was unquestionably thin. We therefore turned aside and skirted the crack for two miles, when it narrowed enough for the dogs to step over it. By that time it was too dark to look for the trail again; so we steered directly for the cabin, as we thought, and in an hour or so reached land. Of the cabin, however, there was no sign, or anything to indicate whether it lay north of us, or south. Thinking that we might have drifted too far to the right, we headed southward, following the flat shore line and halting from time to time to dig through the snow surface in order to ascertain whether we were on land or on sea. For more than an hour we plodded fruitlessly on; then, certain that we were traveling in the wrong direction, we turned and headed north again. The moon was at the half, but its light was dimmed by the foggy atmosphere. In the eerie white haze we wormed our way along, now drifting out to sea and veering back to land again, now floundering over the land in an effort to find the sea edge. Every log of driftwood, every stranded ice cake, helped us by indicating where the shore line lay; but we encountered very few of either, so that our course must have been extremely serpentine.

After four hours of such wandering Brick suggested that we stop, partly unload the sled, and try to sleep on top of it. It was bitterly cold, however, and we possessed no sled cover to shield us from the icy south breeze. So we struggled on, and at 8 P.M. came upon our first recognizable landmark, a low cutbank. Half an hour later the dark outline of the cabin suddenly loomed up on our right, barely discernible through the blanket of fog, although less than fifty yards away. Mechanically we unharnessed and fed the dogs, tied up the animal that was given to straying, and carried our food and bedding indoors. Brick fell fast asleep even before I had the fire well started, and only by vigorous shaking could I awaken him to eat his long-delayed supper.

It was daylight when we rose in the morning, and nearly noon when Brick set out to collect the three traps he had temporarily abandoned in this corner of Harrison Bay. While he was absent I searched out a large driftwood log, and was cutting it up for firewood when Kunarluark's son arrived unexpectedly from the fishing lake, bound, like ourselves, for Cape Halkett, where he had instructions to pick up a supply of blubber. At dusk Brick returned with a fox — his fifth trophy; and right afterward Jim-

112

my and Itarklik appeared, they too driven by an attack of restlessness to visit our neighbors at Cape Halkett. We promptly
elected Jimmy to be both fireman and cook, and while he was
preparing rice and tea, Brick very contentedly skinned his fox.
The arranging of our beds after supper created some confusion,
since the tiny cabin was not designed to shelter five adults. In the
end, however, we all succeeded in stretching ourselves out for the
night, three of us with our heads toward the door, the other two
squeezed in between us with their heads pressing against the back
wall.

Breakfast gave rise to still more confusion. While Jimmy devoted himself to our wood stove Kunarluark's son struggled to
light a primus lamp that he had brought on his sled. Its jet was
clogged, and there was no needle to clean it. Nothing daunted,
Itarklik proceeded to make a needle: he cut a sliver from the
edge of an old baking-powder tin, scraped it down against a log,
and mounted it in a wooden handle. But while he was still labor-
ing with the primus a loud explosion shook the cabin, and one
of the biscuits that Jimmy was deep-frying on the wood stove
jumped right out of the pan, splattering a few drops of seal oil
on the red-hot iron. Immediately an acrid vapor like tear gas
filled the room; it choked our throats and drew streams of water
from our smarting eyes. Three of us fled outdoors; the other two
crouched in a corner until the atmosphere cleared. Itarklik then
took over the boiling of the biscuits and transferred the frying
pan from the wood stove to the hissing primus. Two minutes later
there was a second explosion, the pan dropped to the floor with
a loud clang, and both Itarklik and I leaped simultaneously to
avoid a geyser of scalding oil. When the cabin became habitable
again we put the remainder of the dough in the oven, and break-
fasted on biscuits that were well and thoroughly baked. Then we
loaded up our sleds and moved on toward Cape Halkett.

Only one cabin glimmered in the night as we approached that
little settlement; the second one, Kunarluark's, was dark and
silent, its passageway sealed with snow blocks. We knew that
Kunarluark himself had moved with his family to the fishing

lake; but now his partner Assuark, Brower's brother-in-law, had also moved away and established himself in a cabin ten or twelve miles to the southwestward. Movements such as these seemed to occur quite frequently, because the Eskimos, with the restlessness of nomads in their veins, chafed at long confinement to one small room and to one neighborhood, and always welcomed a change. Moreover foxes, though they never run in packs, probably become more wary after several have lost their lives in one locality; and the hunter who has worked a trap line there for three or four weeks may reasonably expect greater success if he transfers his traps to another area. I tried to learn from the Eskimos how many foxes, approximately, might be expected to visit one locality during the course of a winter, and over how great a territory one fox might roam; but beyond the vague answers "very many" and "very great" they could give me no indication.

Kunarluark's son opened up his family's empty cabin and carried his sleeping bag inside, closely followed by Jimmy and Itarklik with their bags. All three then joined Brick and me in the other house where Aiva, Angopcana's daughter-in-law, treated us to biscuits and tea. Angopcana himself had not yet returned from his trap line, but his blind wife welcomed us graciously, and old Lady McGuire, who was in unusually high spirits, joked with us and corrected my faltering Eskimo. The cabin was illumined as usual by three lamps; on the front wall hung half a dozen brant that were slowly thawing out for breakfast, and near the stove lay a large block of black whale skin on which we dined about 9 P.M. At that repast another guest joined our company, the widower-artist Two Wolves, who had returned unexpectedly to Angopcana's household a few days before, but was leaving in the morning to re-attach himself to Assuark.

After supper Aiva brought out her sewing kit and scrutinized our footwear to see what repairs were necessary. A two-year-old baby toddled around her, grabbing at her knife and anything else that attracted its attention. Some things she allowed it to keep until it lost interest in them; others she gently took away, but immediately soothed the child with an equivalent. Once when she

Aiva

rose and moved toward the doorway to bring in some firewood the baby seized the hem of her parka and checked her steps. The patient mother waited for a full minute before drawing the parka away; then, because the child began to cry, she turned back and played with it until she could slip outside unnoticed. At last the infant fell asleep beside her, and she was free to resume her sewing undisturbed. I noticed, as she skillfully plied her needle, that her wrist possessed the same suppleness as a European woman's, and that the little finger of her right hand separated itself from its neighbor and projected outward, after the manner of many white women drinking tea. It recalled to my memory that in New Guinea also women would flaunt this little finger in the very same way, so perhaps the trait is universal.

Before Two Wolves departed in the morning our generous hosts presented him with a tin of baking powder, some seal blubber, and other supplies which I did not see. He added them to the bedclothes and rifle he had deposited on his hand sled, and was starting out alone, pulling his vehicle behind him, when I suggested that he place it on top of my sled and let the dogs drag the combined load. This he did, and trudged along with us very contentedly for perhaps six miles. Then, in true Eskimo fashion, without a word of thanks or farewell, he turned down a small bay with his hand sled, and we continued on our course.

Another six or seven miles brought us in sight of two rows of fox skins dangling in the air like a Monday laundry and, behind them, two cabins, out of whose passageways several dogs rushed barking as we drew near. Then a man came out, smiled fleetingly, and, grunting "Alapah"—It's cold—hurried inside again. We followed him quickly, and as we passed through the doorway a cross-eyed man ensconced in a corner called me by name and motioned me to occupy the place beside him while the mistress of the house stirred up the fire and put on the kettle. Supper appeared in due course, and we passed a quiet evening, with Brick and the others playing poker while I sat by and watched.

For no apparent reason our hostess rose before five the next morning, and I, who lay as usual near the door, had to turn out of my sleeping bag so that she could go out and come in without stepping over me. Breakfast was so dilatory, nevertheless, that it was eight o'clock before we could hitch up our dogs, and noon when we reached Ukallik, where three months earlier Wilkins and I had found shelter from a blizzard. Arkuvak, our host on that occasion, had been trapping in the locality ever since, and the line in front of his cabin sagged with twenty-one fox skins, a very creditable catch for a man who must have been approaching sixty. He insisted that we remain for lunch, and his wife baked fresh biscuits for us from some flour that we carried indoors. Then a woman entered from the neighboring cabin with more biscuits, and lingered to hear what news we brought from farther up the coast. It was really a very pleasant party, and would have been still pleasanter had I understood more of their language. Just as I rose to leave Mrs. Arkuvak noticed a ripped seam in one of my boots and insisted that I sit down again while she mended it. She might so easily have kept silent and spared herself the trouble, but, being an Eskimo woman, it never entered her mind to shirk any of her responsibilities.

We passed Drew Point and its conspicuous cutbank late in the afternoon. From here our shortest route lay west northwest across the mouth of Smith Bay to Cape Simpson sixteen miles away; but twice already I and my companions had lost our way in this bay, and I felt no desire to repeat the experience. Accordingly we followed the coast line, looking for a cabin reported to lie a little beyond Drew Point. There we proposed to spend the night, and begin the crossing of the bay at daybreak.

We found the cabin without difficulty. Its entrance opened into a small antechamber, and that into a second, both on the same level as the snowbank outside. At the far end of the second chamber a square hole protected by a substantial ledge of snow led down by three steps to the underground passageway and the cabin door. This term "underground" is not strictly accurate, because every cabin and its passageway were built from necessity not under, but on top of the frozen ground, where the walls as well as the roofs stood exposed to the winds during the early part of the winter. Later the drifting snow piled against and over them until by Christmas they were buried beneath a gently sloping mound, six or seven feet deep, that concealed everything except the skylight and the tip of the stovepipe. It then became necessary to cut steps from the entrance of the passageway to the surface of the mound above, and to protect the steps themselves from the drifting snow with a small antechamber, which served also as a storage space.

There were six inmates at this time, a middle-aged man and his wife, and a younger couple with two children aged about six and two. Besides trapping foxes they had set a net in a lake two or three miles away, and were catching so many whitefish as to belie my earlier impression, that this fish becomes sluggish during the midwinter months. They welcomed us cheerfully, despite the smallness of the dwelling, and made room for us in their circle around the tea kettle, the biscuits, and the chunks of frozen fish. The elder man fairly glowed with hospitality: he never ceased to push the biscuits in my direction, and once, when I put down my cup of tea because the liquid was too hot, he picked it up and sampled it to make sure that it was satisfactory. The whole household played cards after supper — all, that is, except the two children, who had fallen asleep against the far wall, and myself, who lay above on the sleeping bench to watch the game. At ten o'clock everyone seemed ready to retire. I then descended from my perch, and after the others had settled in their places, laid out my sleeping bag between the stove and the door.

We were aroused an hour later by the barking of the dogs and the crunching of a sled on the snow outside. My hosts refused to stir from their beds, but I drew on my clothes and, followed by Brick, went out to welcome the traveler, who proved to be a lone man engaged in freighting supplies from Barrow. We shook hands with him, helped him to unload his sled, and, hurrying inside, tumbled into our sleeping bags again. He entered right behind us, to be greeted with the remark that he was too late for supper, but that he might freely help himself to the drinking water he would find in a tin behind the stove. This he did, dipping it up with the cup he had brought with him; and as he slowly sipped the cold liquid, he entered into a lively conversation, telling us what families were now living at Iglora and other places, how many foxes had been caught by various trappers along the coast, and all the latest gossip from Barrow. Not until he had exhausted these topics did he squeeze himself between me and the stove — just how I do not know — and settle down to sleep; and then his distressing cough kept both of us awake until nearly daylight. I suspected that he was suffering from tuberculosis, a malady very prevalent in Alaska at this period. So also was syphilis, another disease that had been introduced by Europeans. One of our Eskimo helpers on board the *Karluk* had contracted it, and the younger of the two women in this cabin bore three or four scars on her back that resembled partly healed syphilitic sores.

This woman and her husband had been planning for several days to journey down to Barrow, and now that Brick and I were traveling thither they decided to accompany us. We left very early in the morning, and, following a firm smooth trail, crossed Smith Bay without mishap. Our companions' six-year-old girl ran or walked beside their sled for the first two miles, but then her mother placed her on top of it and herself mounted my sled, carrying the two-year-old on her back under her warm parka. Pushing on beyond Cape Simpson we reached before dark three houses, two of them empty, the third inhabited by seven adults and one child. We took possession of one of the empty houses which, I discovered later, had been built by Angopcana, who had lingered there for a time during the late fall. It really did not matter who had built it, or occupied it previously, because, as I indicated earlier, the local interpretation of "private property" permitted any man to possess himself without challenge of any cabin that he found empty. He could even vacate it for a time and still retain possession by leaving some of his property in the house, and by carefully sealing the entrance with snow blocks to indicate his intention of returning. But his claim was valid for a short period only; it lapsed if he failed to return within two or three weeks, after which the first comer who needed a cabin was entitled to take it over.

The next day we skirted a line of snowbanks, and after passing two or three high platforms, reached at dark a traditional stopping place named Iglora. Here we found three houses, but the roofs of the two larger ones had collapsed under the weight of the winter snow, and the third was temporarily occupied by a couple with three young sons. Willy-nilly we took shelter in this already crowded cabin, and at bedtime two of us stood outside in the passageway so that the others might have room to arrange their beds. Our host joined us there, and, to fill in the time, inspected a pair of snowshoes that Arlook had made for Brick. He tried them out on his own feet, but being much heavier than Brick, he cracked one of the frames, rendering the snowshoe useless. Had he been a white man he would at once have offered to mend it or to provide another pair. But local custom absolved him from all responsibility. It was an accident; he needed only to express his regret and then forget it. The incident illuminated still further the reservations of the Eskimos on what we consider "private property." It also taught me a useful lesson — never to lend a native any valuable possession, because if he broke it, or lost it, he would not think of replacing it, and would even feel aggrieved if I complained of the loss.

The distance from Iglora to Barrow was only about twenty-five miles, but our dogs were so tired that the journey took us thirteen hours. We halted frequently to rest them, and to give them time to lick away the ice and snow that lodged between their toes and clung in hard lumps to the balls of their feet; otherwise their paws might have frozen, since the thermometer stood at $-32°$ F. Yet it was starvation rather than the cold weather that made them so weary; for some chemical reaction had discolored and hardened the whale blubber we carried for their food, and they either could not, or would not, eat it, but merely sniffed it and turned away. I was glad, for their sake even more than for my own, when we reached Brower's store, because there they would receive plenty of food and be given adequate shelter and rest.

THE WINTER was now well advanced, and everyone was rejoicing at its comparative mildness. On only three or four occasions had the thermometer fallen below —40° F., and those cold spells had been of brief duration. Whether the mildness of the winter affected the foxes I cannot say, but the Eskimos around Barrow had been unusually successful in their trapping, and hardly a day went by without their bringing some trophies to Brower's store. That contented trader purchased his thousandth pelt the day after my arrival, and he was looking forward to doubling the amount by the time the trapping season ended seven weeks later. One might have expected that such an abundance of foxes would be paralled by considerable numbers of polar bears, which could find the same ready supply of food in the frozen whale carcasses stranded along the coast. Up to the middle of February, however, Brower had taken in only seven bear hides, and those of poor quality.

Less than a mile from the trading post stretched the same broad lane of open water that a few months earlier had lured the elderly hunter to try out his fortune with an old-fashioned harpoon. He appeared no longer, but every calm day there came in his place two or three natives dragging kayaks that carried under their deck lashings not only paddles, but long gaffs and Winchester rifles. These more progressive hunters did not harpoon the seals, but shot them from the edge of the ice and retrieved the floating carcasses with their gaffs. Their marksmanship seemed to me rather indifferent, but so abundant were the seals in this locality that they killed a surprising number; on one day alone — admittedly a red-letter day — a single hunter shot nine. During these same weeks other villagers caught a considerable number in square nets made from rawhide, nets strong enough to capture both the ordinary hair seal and the less common but very much larger bearded seal that weighs up to seven hundred pounds. The Alaskan natives have made square sealing nets for at least a thousand years, as we know from the ivory net gauges and fragments of mesh we have discovered in ancient house ruins; yet, strangely enough, they never modified their rawhide nets to catch the fish that are so plentiful in the lakes and rivers, although they knew that their Indian neighbors were using fish nets made from willow bark. It is only during the last two hundred years that the Eskimos have taken to using fish nets, and then their teachers have been not Indians but whites.

The earliest Eskimos must have been, like Nimrod, mighty hunters before the Lord. They probably attacked with their spears even the mammoth, that long-haired elephant which roamed over Arctic Eurasia and Alaska until it became extinct several thousands of years ago. At all events the present-day Eskimos have preserved one or two legends about the ponderous animal, whose bones and tusks they often find lying on the surface of the tundra, or protruding from the weathered banks of the Colville and other rivers. Brower had collected no fewer than twenty tusks that they had brought in to him. The ivory was not as dense as walrus ivory, and commanded little or no value commercially because of its tendency to split; but time had patinated its originally white surface with pleasing shades of orange and pink and chocolate, which variegated the gleam of the polished tusks and untied the purse-strings of a few curio-seekers.

More interesting to me than Brower's mammoth tusks were two cases of archaeological specimens that he had sold to Stefansson the previous October and undertaken to ship to Ottawa as soon as navigation reopened in the coming summer. Every day I spent several hours examining these stone, bone, and ivory objects which the Eskimos had unearthed from ancient dwellings in the vicinity. Brower, who had lived at Barrow for about twenty-five years, could interpret the uses of many; but I learned far more from three old Eskimos who came each morning to brood over the relics of their forefathers and to dream of the years long past. Some objects they knew from tradition only, having themselves never made or used them; a few were as strange to them as to me, and they could not even guess their purpose. I knew, and they knew, that we were peering into a vanished epoch in the history of their race when life had been very different from the life of their childhood. But how could we have suspected, in 1914, that some of their ancestors had turned their backs on the Barrow region a thousand years before and trekked with their sleds toward the sunrise, never looking behind them again until their advance guard, centuries later, reached the Atlantic Ocean at the southernmost tip of Greenland nearly halfway round the globe. Ten more years had to elapse, indeed, before archaeologists began to give serious attention to the Arctic, and to elucidate, chapter by chapter, the intricate and fascinating saga of Eskimo wanderings and achievements during and before the Christian era.

Fuel had not presented any serious problem around Harrison Bay, because the cabins were few and far apart; but the voracious iron stoves of the Barrow settlement had devoured every stick of driftwood within a wide radius, forcing most of the villagers to burn coal brought from Cape Lisburne three hundred miles to the southwest. Building material too was now lacking. Some of the Eskimos were repairing their cabins by appropriating the logs of others that had been abandoned; but all who could afford it were erecting new homes with lumber imported through Brower from the outside. Early each winter they sheathed the walls of these frame houses with symmetrical snow blocks that resembled masonry, and they protected the wooden porches with corridors built either of snow blocks or of blocks of ice sawn from the neighboring lagoon. Ice blocks, of course, were harder to cut than snow blocks, but they were more translucent and neither brushed off on one's clothes nor disintegrated under a sudden knock.

Like myself, Brower had long been wondering why we had received no word from Stefansson, or from the southern party of the expedition which was wintering in Camden Bay three hundred miles east of us. Two messengers, McConnell and an Eskimo, did at last arrive, on February 19. They brought me a letter from Anderson, the leader of the southern party, stating that Stefansson was traveling in the Mackenzie River delta and did not intend to come west to Barrow until he had made an exploratory trip over the sea ice north of Camden Bay. Because his schedule was so indefinite, Anderson strongly advised me to join the southern party without delay, and to pursue my studies in the region around Camden Bay in order that I might be on hand at the opening of the navigation season when the expedition, resuming its original plan, would sail eastward to Coronation Gulf.

One glance at McConnell's dog team showed me how impossible it was to depart immediately. The leader of the team, an extremely intelligent animal, was bleeding from three paws, and had lost most of the hair along one side from frostbite. Four of the other dogs were limping, their feet worn and cut by the pebbly surface of the snow, which was slowly being transformed into ice crystals as the sun rose higher and its rays gathered strength. Every animal in the team needed rest, shelter, good food, and a little doctoring before it would be fit for another journey. Accordingly, I lingered at Brower's nine more days.

During this interval the arrival of mail from the south created a perceptible flutter in the Eskimo community, which carried on a considerable correspondence with Point Hope and other settlements north of Bering Strait. Only the younger generation was literate, and its knowledge of English was still so limited that all letters were written in Eskimo, though with English characters. Every writer necessarily used his own judgment in spelling the Eskimo words, which contain a few sounds that are never heard in English and cannot be properly represented by the characters of our alphabet. No two correspondents therefore spelled the words alike, nor even the same correspondent in two successive letters. However, owing to the structure of the language, which has a multitude of inflections and suffixes, these inconsistencies never seemed to lead to any ambiguity, as they might easily have done in English. Admittedly, the writers did not attempt to discuss the intricacies of the Einstein theory or the adumbrations of Herbert Spencer, but only such everyday subjects as the tally of bears and foxes, the fortunes of a sled party, and the local register of births, deaths, and marriages.

By February 28 McConnell's dogs were sufficiently rested so that they could take the trail again without hardship, provided we covered their feet with "shoes" of sealskin to protect them from the sharp spicules of refrozen snow, and clothed with blankets of caribou fur the two dogs that had lost part of their own fur through frostbite. On that day we drove them twelve miles north to Point Barrow, where we lodged for the night in a large frame house that Brower had built for himself and later turned over to a brother-in-law. It contained three rooms, a living room, a bedroom, and a kitchen, each warmed by a large stove; and it was near the stove in the living room that we lined up our sleeping bags.

The village at Point Barrow was smaller than Barrow itself, but

Two Wolves' sketch of a whale hunt

it occupied a strategic position at the extreme northwest tip of the continent, where it commanded the entrance into the Beaufort Sea, an entrance much narrower than would appear from the map, since the vast, impenetrable fields of ice that fill the polar basin never move far away from the mainland, even in the months of midsummer. The ice pack forced the bowhead whales, which migrated annually from the Pacific into the Arctic Ocean, to follow the water gap along the coast; and it was from the land-attached ice off Point Barrow that the Eskimos intercepted and harpooned them in the late spring.

This whale hunt had once been the most exciting activity of the whole year. Throughout the twenty-four hours of the day, while the sun circled around the sky from south to north and back to south again without touching the horizon, the hunters kept an unbroken watch at the edge of a "lead," ready at any moment to launch their skin-covered boats and hurl their harpoons. There they remained for three or four weeks, neither removing their clothes nor going ashore for a single meal, while back on land their women rigidly observed the time-honored taboos that spelled for their husbands success or failure. One sea monster sixty or eighty feet long would provide food in abundance for many weeks, and in good years the Eskimos had often captured three and even more.

Toward the end of the nineteenth century, however, came white whalers with fleets of small boats and ships equipped with powerful guns; and the number of whales decreased rapidly. Along with the whalers, too, came the fur traders, who, in exchange for fox pelts, replaced with flour and beans and bacon the meat that the Eskimos had derived previously from the whale carcasses. By 1914 the Alaskan Eskimos had completely abandoned whale hunting except at Point Barrow and Point Hope, where a few men still staked their fortunes on it, more from tradition than from real necessity. Brower's brother-in-law was one of these. He invited me to stay with him and join his crew, or rather to share their camp and watch their operations from the edge of the ice; but I dared not linger the two months before the season opened. I heard later that he and his crew killed one whale at the very beginning of the season, but that the lane of water beside which they had been watching then closed over, and did not reopen until the whale migration had passed. Today, both at Point Barrow and at Point Hope, whaling remains a mere memory.

After one night only we left this enterprising outpost and traveled eastward between the sand bars offshore and the mainland, following wherever we could the old sled tracks, although they had been largely obliterated by newly fallen snow. The temperature hovered consistently around —25° F., and a light breeze from the east nipped our cheeks without making them bloodless. Its edge was sharp enough, however, to trouble an Eskimo who crossed our path while he was making the round of his trap line, for it had made him mask with caribou fur both his forehead and his cheeks, which were peeling from frost bite incurred a few days before. We could see nothing of his face except two eyes peering through two narrow slits, and the suggestion of a mouth behind another slit. His mask worked very efficiently, he told us, but for three or four hours only; then moisture from his breath began to congeal inside it until its soft inner layer of fur threatened to become a layer of ice.

Our masked hunter planned to gather up his fox traps the next day, although the official trapping season did not end for another month. Farther on we met other Eskimos who had already taken up their traps and were now traveling down to Barrow to dispose of their furs. One family had mounted a tall mast on the front of its sled, and there its trophies hung like white standards, swinging to and fro with the vehicle's unsteady motion. Every day thereafter we passed one or more cabins that had just been abandoned; their entrances gaped at us silently, and their platforms were gaunt skeletons, stripped to the bare beams. When we halted on the trail to exchange news with their late occupants they told us that the fur catch had fallen off very greatly, either because the animals had become more wary, or because the district had been temporarily trapped out. Yet at the same time they inquired rather eagerly concerning various relatives at Bar-

Lady McGuire

row, and asked about the dances and other activities in that village, which made me suspect that the economic factor was not the sole, or even, perhaps, the main reason for their early exodus, but that they had become more and more oppressed by the loneliness of their trapping existence and could no longer resist the impulse to rejoin their kinsmen.

Not all the cabins that stood empty had been vacated until the next winter. The entrances of two had been closed with snow blocks, cases of what was probably food lay cached on their platforms, and from two poles dangled a score or more fox skins.

It was the latter that particularly caught my attention. Here were what amounted to a year's earnings exposed wide open to the heavens, where the first passerby could appropriate them at his leisure. In reality, of course, they were as safe as in Brower's storeroom, for with a population so small, everyone always knew who was living where, and a pilferer had little or no chance of escaping detection. Human nature the world over is a tissue of weaknesses, and honesty comes much more easily in a tiny community than it does in a great city, where misconduct always hopes that the multitude of alien tracks will cover up its own footprints.

At Halkett we found Angopcana still busily trapping, untroubled by the restlessness that had infected most of the coast, and unperturbed also by the prolonged absence of his partner Kunarluark, who, being short of food, had lingered at the fishing lake and removed his traps to that neighborhood. Lady McGuire almost overwhelmed us with kindness, partly because we were old friends, and partly because Stefansson, who had known her well in earlier years, had sent her, by McConnell, four large caribou hides, the equivalent in European society of a new dress. The old lady was extra gay that evening, and with good reason; for shortly after we arrived one of her granddaughters, whom she had not seen for six months, entered the house unheralded, accompanied by her ten-year-old son. Eskimos seldom display their affection outwardly, although they are as devoted to their families as we are; but they allow the older people to show less reserve than the younger, and certainly not one of them would have criticized this octogenarian great-grandmother who made little or no effort to conceal her tender emotions.

The next morning everyone rose late, and with one delay succeeding another we were unable to leave the settlement until nearly ten o'clock. The customary trail would have led us north along the coast for about two miles, then due east over two lakes in the neck of Halkett Peninsula to the shore of Harrison Bay. Hardly had we started out, however, than we came upon a new trail which headed east immediately and appeared to offer a short cut to that bay. Imprudently we followed it. The sled tracks led us straight for several miles, but then, without warning, they veered sharply south, perhaps toward a fishing lake. By that time it was too late to turn back, so we struggled along in what we presumed to be the right direction, and at 3 P.M. reached sea ice again. This, without question, was our bay. Hopefully we struck out over its open expanse, expecting every moment to encounter the regular trail that would lead us to Arksiatark's cabin; but all too soon we found ourselves stumbling amid darkness and mist, almost invisible to one another and unable to see even one star that might guide us on our course.

To continue on was useless. The dogs were as tired as ourselves. We released them, therefore, and lacking a tent — for McConnell had left his beside mine on Arksiatark's platform, trusting to find shelter in the cabins between there and Barrow — we spread out three caribou hides on the lea side of the sled, laid our sleeping bags on top, and crawled inside without removing either our coats or our footgear. Fortunately there was hardly any wind, or we might have been three corpses in the morning. As it was I dozed fitfully from time to time, and my two companions also enjoyed short intervals of oblivion. But with the first streak of daylight, we crept impatiently out of our cocoons, harnessed up the dogs and moved on, jumping into the air and stamping on the ground to start the blood circulating in our veins again. And within an hour we came upon a sled trail that brought us at noon to Arksiatark's home.

The children were the first to observe our approach. They carried the news inside, and Arksiatark himself came out to welcome us, followed quickly by his wife and Mrs. Arlook. The other members of the household had gone to their trap lines, whence they returned empty-handed just before dark; for here too the foxes were becoming scarcer and scarcer, and the trappers regarded the season as virtually over. Nevertheless, they were tolerably content with their luck, for Arlook had 22 foxes to his credit, and Arksiatark, despite his frequent illness, 9, while Itarklik, who had registered 26 before Christmas when he was trapping at Cape Halkett near the whale carcasses, had now raised that total to 37. Only Jimmy was disgruntled with his meager five, but after all, he was an interloper from another community who had not even begun to trap until the middle of January, and besides he was neither as energetic as his rivals, nor as skillful. He wanted now to borrow a sled and dog team to drive down to Barrow, whence by some means or other he could return to his home at Point

Hope; but neither Arksiatark nor Arlook was anxious to accommodate him, since they still cherished hopes of securing a few more foxes before they sent Itarklik to trade in their furs at Brower's store and themselves awaited the coming of spring at the fishing lake.

Mindful of these two inland Eskimo families when he sent the four caribou hides to Lady McGuire, Stefansson had ordered McConnell to present four hides also to Mrs. Arksiatark and four to Mrs. Arlook, thus repaying the two women in some measure for the hospitality they had accorded me during the winter months. Now it happened that shortly after our arrival Mrs. Arlook noticed that my nose and forehead showed signs of peeling, having been nipped by frost the day before; and, cutting a small patch out of one of her new hides, she proceeded to make me a face mask similar to the mask worn by the Eskimo trapper we had met a few days earlier. Her action could not escape the attention of Mrs. Arksiatark, who earnestly requested me to tell Stefansson that if he should come west in the spring she would gladly perform all the sewing he needed, so grateful was she for the gift he had sent her. "You know," she continued, "he gave Mrs. Arlook and me four skins each, but mine were better than hers. One of hers, in fact, the one from which she is making your face mask, is half-rotten." Everyone in the two rooms could hear her words, but Mrs. Arlook merely kept her head down and said nothing; nor did she pay the slightest attention when her sister-in-law repeated the remark a few minutes later. The two families were planning to travel together throughout the following spring and summer, but I could not help wondering how long they would endure each other's company without a major eruption.

There could be no doubt that the relations between the two women had deteriorated during the winter months. Everyone knew that Mrs. Arksiatark attributed her husband's illness to witchcraft; and though she did not blame Mrs. Arlook openly, a remark she dropped on one occasion convinced me that she believed her sister-in-law could cure his sickness if only she would make full use of her occult powers. All winter Mrs. Arlook had exhibited the patience of Job, but sooner or later one or other of the women would certainly crack under the strain. And when the storm broke, what would become of the child Cookpuck, who seemed to be sheltering more than ever in the room of her aunt and uncle?

Throughout the long winter, it seemed to me, I had been witnessing the opening scenes of a drama that was now hastening toward its denouement. Yet what form that denouement took in the end I cannot say, because barely thirty-six hours after reaching their home we moved on again, leaving the two families my stove and my tent, and dividing between them all the ammunition and supplies that we could spare without jeopardizing our own safety. With their customary pretense at indifference, the men departed for their trap lines even before we had harnessed up our dogs; and neither the women nor the children spoke one word of farewell or came outdoors to see us drive off. Many years have now elapsed since that day, yet not once have I heard from any of them directly, or encountered anyone who could give me news of them.

SPRING was creeping toward the Arctic coast. On March 9, when I left Arksiatark and his people in Harrison Bay, the seven-week-old sun had given us nearly nine hours of daylight; but its rays were still too weak to loosen the grip of winter, and the temperature remained consistently below zero. Four weeks later, however, the sun was traveling in a higher arc, and its rays, more direct and shining five hours longer, were changing the white blanket around us into a glittering gray sheet as the grains of snow on its surface slowly melted and refroze into granules and spicules of pure ice. On April 6 the thermometer hovered around 30° F., drawing down streams of water from the snow-covered roofs of tents and houses, and exposing here and there some light-colored boulder or small patch of brown soil. It is true that the temperature fell precipitately to —15° F. again, a drop of 45° F. in only twenty-four hours; but for two weeks thereafter the soft snow, varying in depth from six inches to two feet, rendered traveling difficult, since the hard crust that formed on its surface was too thin and too weak to bear the weight of either man or dog. By the end of April, this crust too had melted, large pools of water had gathered on top of the sea ice, and on the land little rivulets were coursing and bounding in all directions. After the frozen silence of the long dark winter, the bubbling laughter of these rivulets was as cheerful and hope-inspiring as the warm rays of the ever-mounting sun.

Other signs of spring soon manifested themselves. During the last week of April the sun did not set until about 9:30 P.M., and between that hour and 2:30 A.M., when it appeared again, there was no real darkness, but a constant glow as of sunrise. Two weeks earlier we had seen our first rain clouds since the previous autumn, a build-up of cumulo-nimbus near the western horizon, with alto-cumulus overhead; it promised us rain, not snow, but we had to wait another month for our first Arctic drizzle. The ocean too was awakening. More and more often we began to see to the northward a heavy black line where the sea ice had cracked wide open and a dark lane of water was casting its shadow on the sky above.

Nature was stirring everywhere. The herds of caribou that had found shelter and food throughout the winter among the passes of the Brooks Range west of the international boundary were beginning to move down toward their summer pastures near the coast; already they had lost three score of their number to keen-eyed Eskimo hunters. On days of bright sunshine a few seals crawled out of their breathing holes to bask on the surface of the sea ice; but the majority still lingered below it, waiting for warmer weather. The ptarmigan were changing to their summer plumage; their necks had turned brown, though their bodies preserved the winter white. And the lemmings, which for seven months had been whiter than the snow in which they burrowed, also heard the call of spring and set about transforming their coats, beginning not with the neck, like the ptarmigan, but with the body, where they sent out a brown stripe right down the spine.

With the opening of May the signs of spring multiplied. Out on the sea ice, black specks became more numerous as more and more seals sought the warm sun; and on land the patches of brown soil grew in size and number, encouraging a few marmots

Eskimo drawing of caribou

to emerge from their holes. New birds began to arrive from the south. The only species that had dared to face the rigorous winter were the ptarmigan, the raven, and the white or snowy owl; but on May 3 I heard the twittering of snow buntings, and a few days later three geese flew over my head. On May 14 the weatherman actually sent us a few raindrops, although he quickly decided that the season was still too early and changed the rain to snow again.

The Eskimos, being themselves products of this environment, necessarily conformed to its rhythm. In April some of the Point Barrow Eskimos were camped on the sea ice, intent on intercepting the whales that were tortuously working their way into the Arctic Ocean. Arksiatark and Arlook were probably at the fishing lake, since the trapping season had ended on March 31; or perhaps they were already moving up the Colville River to their summer fishing and hunting grounds somewhere on the divide between that river and the Noatak. Farther east, behind our expedition's base in Camden Bay, a larger band of Nunatarmiut Eskimos, sixty or more in number, who had wintered on the south side of the Brooks Range around the headwaters of the Chandelar River, were now crossing those mountains and descending the Hulahula River to the seacoast, in order to sell their furs to one or another of the trading vessels that were lying frozen-in offshore, or that would skirt the coast during the approaching season of open water. And from the Mackenzie River delta an-

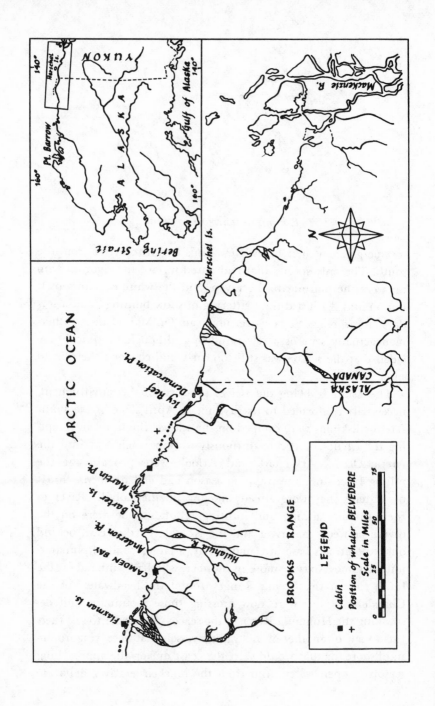

other stream of Eskimos was pouring westward over the international boundary line, lured not only by the abundance of seals there, but also by the hope of obtaining from those same trading vessels higher prices for their furs and services than were being offered by the trader of the Hudson's Bay Company at Herschel Island.

Actually no season of the year was more favorable for journeying by sled. The twenty-four hours of continuous daylight had erased time's usual punctuations of morning, noon, and night, so that the traveler could roam along at his leisure, unoppressed by any feeling of haste, or by the necessity to reach some suitable camping site before dark. Indeed night travel — if I may still use the word "night" — was really preferable to day travel, because with the slight lowering of the temperature between 6 P.M. and 6 A.M. the surface of the ice became less slushy and the sled glided along more easily. Fog was rather improbable, since the ocean and the land were still nearly alike in temperature; only toward the end of May, and in June, would it become prevalent, after the land had lost most of its snow cover and was absorbing some of the heat of the never-setting sun. Rivers offered no obstruction, inasmuch as they would remain frozen for another month, even though it was warmer in the mountains than on the coast.

The traveler could count on a few snow flurries, but these he would shrug off with a laugh, remembering the fierce blizzards and subzero temperatures of the real winter. Under no circumstances, however, would he now omit to wear goggles to protect his eyes from the intense glare, for snow blindness is both crippling and exceedingly painful; and he would inspect the canvas or hide shoes of his dogs at frequent intervals, replacing them with others before they wore through and allowed the dogs' feet to be cut to ribbons on the sharp ice spicules. He himself needed special spring boots with strong soles, although most of the pools left by the melted snow drained away quickly through holes and cracks in the sea ice. Even with special boots his feet were generally soaking after the first two hours; but wet feet no longer meant cold feet, or feet that were in danger of freezing, and with the abundant driftwood on shore he could dry out his boots and socks at the end of each day's march. There were patches of dry ground everywhere for his camp site, and no mosquitoes as yet to patter on his tent like raindrops, or to flutter up and down in clouds like the motes in a sunbeam. He could eat when he liked, sleep when he liked, enjoy the warm sunshine without a single care, and let the hours slip by him.

Nevertheless, pleasant as seemed this prospect, when spring first made its appearance in early April, I myself had no desire to start traveling again. The journey from Barrow to our expedition's base in Camden Bay had been long and tedious, interrupted more than once by very unfavorable weather. On one occasion — two nights after we left Arksiatark's home — a sudden eighty-mile-an-hour squall brought the tent and stovepipe tumbling about our ears, rousing us from a well-earned sleep. I had to plant my feet desperately, like Atlas, to hold up our little world while McConnell and our Eskimo companion struggled to readjust the guy ropes; in the morning we labored nearly an hour digging out the tent from under the four-feet-high snow drifts, and uncovering the sled, which was buried to the tips of the handle bars. Later, most of our dogs became worn out and crippled; one we released from its harness for two days to give it a chance to recover, but another collapsed outright and we had to shoot it where it lay. This animal should never have been brought into the far north, because its own fur was too short to protect it from the bitter weather, and the caribou-fur robe we wrapped round its body was not an adequate substitute. Sled dogs rarely find a place in history books, but it is generally they and not men who are the real heroes of the Arctic.

It was perhaps excusable, therefore, that I should rest awhile at the expedition's base in Camden Bay, where I was experiencing more comfort than I had known all winter. The nucleus of the base was a large log cabin built a year or two before by a white trader; around it were grouped supply tents, quarters for the dogs, caches of ammunition, a miniature observatory, and sundry other constructions. Near by, in the bay, were our two schooners, the *Alaska* and the *Mary Sachs,* firmly embedded in the ice, which was there about five feet thick. The scientific members of the expedition occupied bunks inside the log cabin, but at this period all of them were absent except Dr. Anderson; and he too departed presently for the mountains, being anxious to collect some zoological specimens within their folds before the rivers broke out and made traveling temporarily impossible. Before his departure he delegated the captain of the *Alaska* to take charge of the camp, so that I might be completely free to come and go as I wished, to pore over my notes of the previous winter, and to browse among the books of the small library that had been supplied to us before we left civilization. I found in that library a mutilated German-Eskimo grammar of the Labrador dialect which happily resolved several linguistic problems that had troubled me earlier; and I spent many profitable hours working at the Eskimo language, and interrogating three Eskimos who were then employed at our base, Fred, Billy Natkusiak, and Jennie Thompson.

Fred had been my faithful if somewhat dull-witted companion on the journey from Barrow. He came from the old gold-mining town of Nome, and spoke a dialect so different from that of the Arctic-coast Eskimos that only with difficulty did they understand one another. When conversing with the white members of the expedition, of course, he used English, which he spoke very ungrammatically, but with startling fluency. Of the manners and beliefs of his ancestors he knew very little, having lived all his life in the vicinity of whites; but he could speak of the once-prevalent custom of infanticide from his own personal experience. He was the youngest of four children, he said, and unwelcomed by his parents, who resolved to destroy him on the very day that he was born. His mother, accordingly, pushed him inside a sack, and pressed her whole weight on him to crush the life from his body; but he was still breathing when she drew him out again. Thereupon his father relented and said, "Well, if the child wants to live let it live"; and they raised him with the other children. "Ever since," Fred added, "my chest, as you can see, has not been as strong as it should be." I did not see. To me, he appeared as strong as an ox. Only rarely on the journey from Cape Smythe had he confessed to the slightest fatigue.

Billy Natkusiak, a newcomer at the base, was an Eskimo of very different stamp, more adventurous, and more self-sufficient. I met him first on our journey east when, following a sled trail three days out from Harrison Bay, we arrived at his rectangular dwelling built not from logs, but from snow blocks overlain with poles and roofed with a large canvas. A short passageway of snow blocks protected the door, which was nothing more than the hide of a grizzly; and inside there was little to be seen except a kerosene-tin stove, two pots and a frying pan, a box of food and sundries, and, at the back, a rough flooring of logs under a pile of caribou hides. Soon afterward Billy himself came stamping in from his trap line, which extended for about forty miles along the coast, here totally uninhabited. He told us, over the evening meal, that he had pre-empted this locality a few weeks before Christmas after finding a whale carcass stranded offshore on a mud flat, where it was providing three polar bears with their daily meal; and he congratulated himself on choosing so fertile a trapping ground, since he had garnered during the winter no fewer than forty-two foxes. However, now that the season was practically over, he intended to take up his traps and follow us to Camden Bay so that he could enter our service.

It seemed rather amazing that he should have lived alone throughout the whole winter, fifty miles from his nearest neighbor, without a woman to cook his meals, patch his boots, or sew up the rents in his clothing. To be sure, an Eskimo cookbook, if such a work existed, would contain no more than two or three recipes, none of which would require a long apprenticeship; and as for the clothing, Billy himself could mend it quite skillfully with sinew thread and a steel needle. No doubt some woman had cut out and fitted his garments in the first place, he himself probably supplying the skins. But why had he remained unmarried, a condition so alien to the normal Eskimo way of life? He was a good-looking man of about thirty, well built and with no visible defects that would detract from his eligibility as a husband; and

Jennie and baby Annie

he was an excellent hunter and trapper, the chief quality demanded by every prospective bride, or at least by her parents. Moreover he was a cheerful fellow who seemed easy to get along with, rather happy-go-lucky indeed, with a twinkle always lurking in his dark brown eyes. Were his boots wet? He would dry them in due course. Was there blubber on his clothing? Oh well, he would get new clothes perhaps in the autumn. Apparently he was one of those philosophers who agree with Candide that everything is for the best in the best of all possible worlds.

I suspect that one reason for his celibacy was his insatiable wanderlust; another that he lacked fixed roots in this region, for he had been brought up, not on the Arctic coast, but at Port Clarence, a little south of Bering Strait. What first attracted him to the country between Barrow and the Mackenzie delta I did not discover, but Stefansson had met him there during his 1908–11 expedition and had promptly hired him for a journey to Victoria Island, a thousand miles to the eastward. Billy greatly admired Stefansson's prowess as a hunter and traveler; and he loved to relate anecdotes of their joint adventures among the primitive Eskimos to the east, very few of whom at that time had ever seen a white man or possessed the slightest knowledge of the outside world and its strange inventions.

By his own confession, Billy himself had posed among them as a great magician. He would light his pipe with a little stick (match), inhale the smoke, and after a pause blow it out through his nostrils, telling his audience that there was fire inside his body. In one settlement he frizzled some doughnuts in a pan of boiling seal oil and invited the curious onlookers to partake of the new meat. Two or three of the boldest did break off small fragments hardly larger than a pin's head and gingerly swallow them; others carried off tiny pieces to their families so that they too might view the strange food. "I laugh all the time I there," added Billy. "One time they ask me what my woolen shirt and I tell them raven skin. Stefansson say, 'What this lie you tell them?' and I say, 'Oh, that all right.'"

Billy knew too much to be of great assistance to me, but Jennie

Thompson, who came from Fred's birthplace, Nome, was less sure of herself and more helpful. Like Mrs. Arlook she was a hunchback; and she possessed the same quiet voice and patient smile. Our expedition had engaged her as seamstress when it recruited her white husband as seaman; and in Camden Bay it had assigned them private living quarters on board the *Mary Sachs*. Now that the base was half-deserted, however, Jennie, carrying her sixteen-month-old baby on her back, came ashore every day about noon to spend the hours until bedtime in our big log cabin; for she felt cramped and lonely inside the schooner's narrow hull, especially since her husband spoke no Eskimo and she herself had acquired only a smattering of English. Not that she was ever depressed or ill-humored, for an Eskimo woman demands very little: her world is small and her mental horizon limited. Life seems full and satisfactory to her if she has someone who will supply her basic needs of food and shelter, someone for whom she must cook and sew and by whom, in due course, she can bear two or three children. Travel by sea and land, visits to and from other Eskimos, and an occasional ceremony or dance, these are welcome diversions necessary to prevent too great monotony. But her proper mission, she believes, is to establish and maintain a smoothly running household; and she would endorse with little question Hitler's terse summary of woman's functions, merely changing the order of *küche* and *kinder*, and leaving out the *kirche* altogether.

At this period of her married life Jennie's whole universe revolved about her baby Annie, for whom she had recently borrowed a six-year-old child as nursemaid. The nursemaid's mother had long since died and her reputed father, Terigloo, was living with his family at the base camp of an American geologist named Leffingwell thirty-five miles to the west of us. When I stopped there for the night on the journey from Barrow, Leffingwell had been absent in the mountains, rounding off six years of field explorations with one last sled trip before returning to the United States. His caretaker Terigloo, however, had shown himself a very satisfactory host, and the relations I established with him on that occasion became much more intimate later.

Terigloo's "Kanaka" daughter

His "daughter" and baby Annie were romping inside our cabin one evening when the elder child suddenly sneezed. "Kakatkain," cried Jennie, and smiled at me when I looked up questioningly. "Is it the atka?" I asked her; and she replied, "Yes, it is the namesake spirit informing us of its presence. We always answer 'kakatkain' so that it may know that it is welcome."

The little nursemaid's appearance puzzled me; she possessed the broad face and slightly oblique eyes of a typical Eskimo child, but her skin was unusually dark, and her black hair, unlike that of any other Eskimo I had seen, was frizzly. When I questioned Jennie about her parentage she told me that the mother was an Eskimo woman, and the real father a "Kanaka" from a whaling vessel. The whaling vessels that visited the Beaufort Sea carried not only Polynesians from the Hawaiian Islands to whom the word "Kanaka" might rightly apply, but also Cape Verde Islanders of Negro or mixed Portuguese-Negro ancestry; and the shape of the child's hair indicated that it was Negro and not Polynesian blood that flowed in her veins. Happily there was no prejudice against her on that account, or she would not have been so merry — the merriest child, indeed, along the whole coast. But I wondered whether the physical type of many other Eskimos in the northwestern Arctic had not been considerably modified by the crews of whaling ships, which had been operating in this region for nearly half a century.

The most important member of Jennie's household, her husband Thompson, I met only casually until the day when he accidentally crossed the path of a polar bear. With other crew members of the *Alaska* and *Mary Sachs* he had laid down a few fox traps at the beginning of winter; and he had been the luckiest of them all, having captured to date twenty-four foxes. Then on March 29, only two days before the season ended, he left the base about 9 A.M. to make the customary circuit of his traps, while the rest of us occupied ourselves with various tasks. At noon he reappeared, half-running, half-stumbling, his face ashen, his breath coming in short gasps. One of his traps, it seemed, had been planted on a small mound four miles away; but when he had approached within a few yards of it a huge polar bear sprang to its feet and growled at him. The shotgun he was carrying was worse than useless. He did the wisest thing he could have done — he turned and ran, but not before he had glimpsed a small white object in his trap, whether fox or bear cub he could not distinguish.

Three of us seized our rifles and returned with him, less interested in the fox trap than in the prospect of securing some fresh meat, which we had lacked for several weeks. We sighted the bear from a mile away; it was pacing restlessly up and down, pausing every now and then to stare in our direction. It paused more frequently as we drew nearer, and at last faced us squarely with a challenging roar. Between its legs lay a cub hardly larger than a fox, caught in the trap by one leg and unable to tear itself free; and the mother would not abandon it, even when outnumbered by her deadliest enemies. We shot them both — sheer butchery, of course, but we needed the meat, and the cub would have died in any case. Thompson claimed their skins in compensation for the fright he had received.

This episode made able-seaman Thompson the second member of our expedition who had involuntarily played tag with a bear. Ten months earlier, while our flagship *Karluk* was lying at anchor in Port Clarence awaiting the arrival of Stefansson from Nome, one of our sportsmen-scientists had wandered inland to look for ptarmigan and, shotgun in hand, mounted to the summit of a ridge from one side at the very moment when an enormous grizzly breasted it from the other. The two "hunters" faced each other in amazement. Then both turned and fled, one east, the other west, and the scientist did not stop running until he reached the ship again.

But grimmer episodes were not lacking, for tragedy in one shape or another is forever stalking the Arctic. It invaded even our base at Camden Bay, where the cook suffered so many hallucinations during the early part of the winter that the staff kept a quiet watch on his movements. On Christmas Eve he slipped away from the house unnoticed and did not return. Seven or eight men searched for him all the next day but failed to discover him

Eskimo drawing of polar bear

until the third morning, when they came upon him slowly plodding back to the base, his cheeks and chin severely frozen. It seemed a miracle that he had survived seventy-two hours of exposure to temperatures of $-30°$ F. and even lower; but apparently he had sheltered his hands and wrists inside his trousers by withdrawing his arms from the sleeves of his coat, and he had maintained the circulation of his blood by ceaseless walking.

For several weeks after this experience he seemed quite normal, but late in March he again began to act strangely. He would sit silent for an hour at a stretch, gazing blankly in front of him, or picking up some object and laying it down again as though unable to focus his mind on anything. Once while sawing wood outside the house he burst into tears and, approaching the captain of the *Alaska*, asked piteously, "Have I done anything to you?" The next night, after most of us had undressed and climbed into our bunks, he put on a heavy coat, took up a shotgun, and was disappearing into the darkness when someone intercepted him and asked where he was going. "I am going to look at my traps," he answered, although we all knew that he possessed no traps. We persuaded him to postpone his inspection until the morning, and one of us stood beside him until he was safely in bed. By morning, of course, he had forgotten the matter entirely.

Easter Sunday, April 12, passed without incident. Four mornings later I went outdoors before breakfast to read the thermometers and the wind gauge; and as I re-entered the dark passageway, half-blinded by the bright light outside, I almost collided with a shadowy figure that suddenly blocked my way. A murmur reached my ears, "You nearly bumped into me," and I recognized the voice of the cook. Groping past him I entered the house, and, after holding the door ajar for a moment in case he was following, let it close quietly behind me. At that same instant a loud bang resounded from the passage, and when I flung open the door again, I discovered him prone on the ground, his head shattered, his right hand still clutching a rifle.

We buried him on a low knoll half a mile east of our camp, and planted a small cross over his grave. He was only fifty-two years of age, and, judging from my brief acquaintance with him, kind and rather gentle. But he had suffered many hardships in Alaska, and in the end they undermined his sanity.

During the first half of April we entertained a youngish, quiet-spoken Eskimo named Ayacook who had married a widow ten years his senior and adopted as his own her two teen-aged sons. Like Billy Natkusiak, he was a native of another region; but he had lived here from boyhood and explored the whole coast line from Barrow to the Mackenzie delta. While trapping the past winter near Barter Island, about fifty miles east of our base, he had noticed a large number of ruined dwellings, some very close to his camp, others a few miles distant. The majority still lay hidden beneath the snow; but a few were now visible, and he would gladly show them to me if I were interested in examining them.

His visit occurred at a time when my linguistic studies with Jennie and Fred, though interesting and rewarding, had begun to pall a little, and the bright sun that peered through our hut window was calling me outdoors more and more insistently. Was there not useful archaeological work that I could perform in this area? Had the Eskimos ever built permanent settlements here, settlements comparable to those at Barrow and Point Barrow which they occupied winter and summer alike? Franklin had seen only summer residents when he explored the coast line in 1826, and Collinson, who wintered in Camden Bay twenty-five years later while searching for traces of Franklin, did not come upon any permanent settlement in its neighborhood. The Nunatarmiut Eskimos whom we daily expected to arrive at the coast spent all their winters in the mountains; but whether their forefathers had also wintered there before the days of the fur trade, or whether some had remained on the coast to track down the seals at their breathing holes while others fished and hunted caribou in the interior, no one seemed able to tell me. Perhaps the ruins that Ayacook had reported would resolve some of these problems if I dug into them during the coming summer. At all events they were worth examining; and besides it would be pleasant to start tramping again, now that the winter had broken. I told him, therefore, that I would first reconnoiter the shores of Camden Bay, and after a week or two, when more of the snow had melted and more ruins become visible, would run down to his camp to inspect the sites in its vicinity.

The shores of Camden Bay proved barren. I found ruins of three or four houses, but all so recent that in one case at least Terigloo could recall the name of its owner. Their walls and roofs had collapsed, forming low hummocks that were still covered with snow; but the logs that protruded from them seemed as sound as the day they had been set up. There may have been older dwellings whose frames had completely decayed, leaving only the barest outlines; but if so, they were concealed and invisible.

From every excursion along the bay I returned with wet feet because the temperature, while averaging close to zero over the twenty-four hours of the day, rose high enough in the early afternoon to convert the snow into slush, which penetrated my winter boots as if they were blotting paper. Jennie Thompson observed my plight, and set about making me a pair of spring boots that would protect me from such discomfort. She used for the feet the thick hide of the bearded seal, scraped clean of all hair and soaked in seal oil to render it waterproof; and for the uppers, hide from caribou legs likewise soaked with oil. Most spring boots had uppers of sealskin with the hair turned out; but Jennie knew that I felt the cold more keenly than the Eskimos, and thoughtfully substituted the warmer caribou fur. She supplied for them, too, insoles of grass that could be taken out and dried each evening, since however tightly the boots were tied at the knees, some water or moisture always crept in through their seams. She might indeed have made me regular water boots of tanned sealskin in which I could have waded for hours without wetting my feet; but they would have been less warm than the spring boots and necessitated more exact and painstaking sewing.

Equipped with my new footgear, I threw my sleeping bag and a little food on top of a light sled, harnessed three dogs, and drove away in the direction of Ayacook's camp. Scarcely a breath of air was stirring that morning, and the sun shone so brightly that it was hard to believe the thermometer registered two or three degrees below zero. To the southward the Brooks range of mountains framed the horizon starkly; the black ridges separating its snow-filled valleys resembled the thin midribs of a row of white leaves. My dogs, well rested and well fed, seemed to enjoy the outing, and sped along so lightly that from time to time I gladly checked their pace by adding my own weight to the sled. I passed, shortly after noon, the mouth of the Sadlerochit River, near whose headwaters a hunting party from our base had discovered a hot spring; and by 6 P.M. I drew near the log cabin in which the engineer of the *Alaska* had spent the second half of the winter, redeeming its dreary days from idleness by trying out his luck with eight or ten fox traps. Many ptarmigan tracks pitted the soft snow where the birds had been feeding on the grass tops, but no fox pelts fluttered from the line outside his hut, because he had taken up his traps two days before my arrival and was now putting together his possessions so that he could return to his vessel and overhaul the engine.

From this cabin to Ayacook's camp on Arey Island was only a half-day's run. I found him living not in a log hut, but in a large rectangular tent walled in with snow blocks that concealed everything except the roof and the stovepipe projecting above it. The interior seemed warm and almost cheerful with the sunlight diffusing through the white walls; but I suspect it had been gloomy and uncomfortable during the months of the real winter. His

The billowing sail

stepsons had taken his sled and driven north to shoot seals in a lane of open water whose reflection we could see in the sky, but Ayacook himself had shrewdly remained at home, suspecting — as proved to be the case — that the water lane was many miles away and only seemed near through an atmospheric mirage. He gladly showed me the house ruins half a mile from his tent, then guided me over the ice to the neighboring Barter Island, where we inspected two old settlements, one on its western sandspit and the other on the eastern.

Barter Island owes its name to the explorer Sir John Franklin, in whose day it seems to have been a trading rendezvous; for he writes, "The Western Esquimaux having purchased the furs from those men that dwell near the Mackenzie, at Barter Island, proceed to the westward again without delay." Franklin does not record its Eskimo name, but toward the end of the nineteenth century the local natives called it *karktorvik*: "the place where people use a seine." Then and later it was a popular fishing place, which could adequately account for the name, but Ayacook in-

sisted on explaining it by a rather fantastic story about a dis-
tracted father who, after a long search, discovered the body of his
murdered son caught in the meshes of his own fishing net.

Snow still mantled the surface of each site to which Ayacook
led me, but the patches of brown earth that mottled it disclosed a
multitude of ruins, not all, apparently, of the same age. On the
west end of Barter Island, for example, a straightening of the
walls and roof of one dwelling, and a renewal of its turf insulation, would have rendered it habitable again, whereas nothing
was visible of another dwelling only thirty yards away except two
badly decayed posts. Ayacook told me that during the previous
summer Terigloo had ransacked some of the ruins and sold the
"curios" to the crew of a trading vessel; he had found no trace of
iron in them, so that they were certainly a hundred years old, and
might easily be more than two hundred. We ourselves could not
hope to excavate any of them for at least five or six weeks, since
even the crust of the frozen ground was as hard as granite, and
the frost extended to unmeasured depths beneath. I therefore
arranged that both Ayacook and his elder stepson should dig
with me as soon as the upper surface thawed, and in the meantime I would search for more ruins farther east.

The return trip to Camden Bay was as pleasant as the outward
journey. After spending a night with the engineer I loaded his
goods onto my sled and started homeward with him, rejoicing in
the brisk wind that fanned our backs. "Why not make use of the
wind?" he suggested. We halted the dogs, lashed a short mast to
the prow of the sled, attached to the mast the square of canvas
that protected his bedroll, and moved on again. The bellying sail
lifted the sled's prow and drove it onward so swiftly that we could
hardly keep abreast of it; and even when we threw ourselves on
top and added our weight to its load it still threatened each
moment to overrun the fleeting dogs. However, the breeze died
down an hour later, the animals' nerves and tempers subsided,
their passengers dismounted, and men and dogs in harmony proceeded at a more dignified pace toward our base.

TWO DAYS after my return to Camden Bay a party made ready to freight a supply of gasoline to the Mackenzie delta for the use of our geologist and topographers, who were to survey its waterways as soon as the ice broke out. This seemed to me an excellent opportunity to reconnoiter any archaeological sites that might lie between Barter Island and Demarcation Point, the Arctic Ocean terminus of the boundary line that separates Alaska from Canada. At Demarcation Point I would find a combined store and cabin that Stefansson had recently bought from an itinerant white trader (who had promptly pocketed his check and hurried out to civilization); and I could make that cabin my home until another sled appeared that would carry my sleeping bag westward again.

We left the base on April 26. The heavily laden sled traveled slowly, so that I was able to skirt the shore line while it crossed from headland to headland. Here and there I came upon an isolated ruin, and at two places beyond Barter Island two dilapidated cabins together; but all were too recent to warrant much attention. Tragedy seemed to have overtaken one pair of cabins, because a pile of logs on a nearby knoll covered a comparatively fresh grave — covered but did not protect it, for foxes had wormed their way in and torn to shreds the caribou-fur shroud. We spent our second night at Martin Point, the most conspicuous projection on the mainland between Point Barrow and the Mackenzie delta, and about 4 P.M. the following day stopped for lunch at the *"Polar Bear* Camp" just ten miles beyond.

The *Polar Bear* was a diesel-driven schooner about seventy feet long, commanded by an experienced Arctic navigator who had planned to trade along the coast of Siberia on each side of Bering Strait before rounding Point Barrow. To defray some of his expenses he had contracted with three wealthy Bostonians to land them on Banks Island at the beginning of the navigation season, and to take them off at its close, after they had spent the intervening weeks hunting caribou and other game. Two biologists had then joined the ship to collect Arctic specimens for their respective museums. Neither they nor anyone else had anticipated that the vessel might be trapped by ice before it ever reached Banks Island; yet here it was, frozen in between Martin Point and Icy Reef. Near it, but farther out to sea, a second schooner, the *Elvira,* had been simultaneously frozen in; but she had been sunk or carried away by the same storm that carried away our flagship *Karluk.* That storm would have carried away the *Polar Bear* also had she not been imprisoned in shallow water near the coast, where the ice surrounding her rested on the sea bottom and withstood the pressure of the gale without moving. The vessel thus survived, and after the danger had passed her crew, conveying most of her supplies ashore, erected a comfortable log cabin, in which half of them passed the winter while the others remained on board.

The winter, however, had been long and wearisome, and the Bostonians, not interested in anything the Arctic could offer except big game hunting, became more and more depressed. On the day we lunched with them one man had gone out with a shotgun and returned with a brace of ptarmigan; but his companions could hardly muster enough energy to walk six paces in the open

The Belvedere

air, despite the bright sunshine and mild weather. The two biologists, on the other hand, had been collecting specimens out of doors, and studying them inside the hut, from early morning until bedtime. But specimens were still scarce, because spring had hardly begun; so when a rumor reached them that the season was more advanced, and spring birds more in evidence, at Demarcation Point, they had packed their bags and hastened thither only four days ahead of me.

The Bostonians hospitably shared their lunch and even invited me to stay over for a few days; but they were unable to promise me any ruins. We therefore pushed on, and after a twelve-mile run came to a much larger vessel that was also locked in the ice, the whaling steamer *Belvedere*, of approximately 3000 tons. Twenty years earlier her bow had been sheathed with Australian ironbark, and though she had buffeted the polar ice every summer since, and during the last summer had rammed a floe so hard that it broke part of her stem, the ironbark showed scarcely a scratch on its surface and appeared as sound as the day it was cleated on. For her commander, Captain Cottle, this was the twenty-sixth voyage into the Arctic, the last ten of them shared by his wife. Each August and September he had scoured the Beaufort Sea for bowhead whales, whose baleen still commanded a considerable price; and later, toward spring, he had crisscrossed the North Atlantic between the Cape Verde Islands and the West Indies, hunting the more valuable sperm whales. At my request he penciled on a chart his favorite area for sperms, a tract in mid-ocean that centered around 12° north latitude and 140° west longitude.

His was a hard life, and a hazardous one, yet the portly Mrs. Cottle seemed contented to share it. She was a very placid woman, unconscious of, or at least undisturbed by, any of the rough episodes that must inevitably occur on a whaler. It was her invariable placidity, I suspect, that had mellowed the character of the captain himself, for under a reserved exterior he was quite a genial man, not at all the blaspheming, hardfisted whaling skipper of Jack London fame. Just the same he was a strict disciplinarian, as indeed he needed to be with a crew as motley as any that ever sailed the seven seas. It included a cockney from London and a "bluenose" from Nova Scotia, United States citizens of both white and colored ancestry, Portuguese and Portuguese Negroes from the Cape Verde Islands, two Russians, seven Eskimos from Indian Point on the coast of Siberia, and an undetermined number of others whose nationalities were presumably just as varied.

It was the captain's custom at the beginning of each Arctic cruise to call at some place on the Asiatic coast and to hire there as many Eskimos as would sign on with him; for he maintained that the Siberian Eskimos were better workers than the Alaskan, although he knew no reason for the difference. I noticed that the speech of his Siberians differed considerably from the Barrow dialect that I had been learning, and that they often failed to understand or be understood by their American cousins. This was the more surprising because at that period the two groups frequently crossed Bering Strait to trade with one another, and both archaeology and tradition agreed that the traffic was not new, but dated back many generations. It persisted indeed even after the Bolshevik revolution, for in the summer of 1926, while I was excavating some ruins at Wales, on the American side of the strait, an umiak manned by Siberian Eskimos called there on its way to Nome to purchase supplies, and called again on the return trip. One of its crew then told me, in a queer Eskimo-English jargon, that fighting had broken out near his home between what I assumed to be Soviet Russians and White Russians. Although it was impossible to confirm his report, some disturbance probably did occur about that time, because since 1926 not a single boatload of Siberian natives has made its way over to the Alaskan side, nor have any Alaskan natives crossed over to Siberia. And during this last quarter of a century immense changes have taken place on both coasts, so that whenever the strait is opened again to cross-traffic — as it surely must be some day — both the merchants and the goods will have altered almost beyond recognition.

It may appear strange — though not if we consider the stream of pearls and diamonds that flows today from Europe to America — that the most valued objects carried by the Siberian Eskimos to Alaska in prehistoric and early historic times were not tools and weapons of iron or other metal, but blue beads about the size of marbles, occasionally made from real turquoise, but generally from glass. Where they were manufactured I cannot say, but the Eskimos nearly always split them in two (unless they received them so split) and mounted each half, like a jewel, on an ivory stud or labret which the owner "buttoned" through a perforation at the corner of his mouth. I found two of these half-beads in the archaeological collection at Barrow that Brower had sold to Stefansson; and an old Eskimo there told me that he could remember when their leading man paid, for one half only, a sled and six dogs, ten slabs of baleen (at a time when baleen had reached its highest price), about fifty white-fox pelts, six cross-fox pelts, and sundry other goods, making a total amount which, translated into terms of our economy, would approach the value of the Cullinan diamond. These blue beads quickly lost their value in the second half of the nineteenth century, when the whalers and white traders introduced substitutes, and when the Eskimos themselves, acquiring more utilitarian ideas, hastened to equip themselves with rifles and shotguns.

The Asiatic and Alaskan Eskimos had generally met in one of two bays where, by mutual agreement, they temporarily laid aside their blood feuds and observed a strict armistice during the period of trading. Sometimes the Alaskans went to Kolyuchin Gulf on the Siberian coast northwest of Bering Strait; more often the Siberians crossed over to Kotzebue Sound in Alaska, a place that was frequented in summer by natives from farther up the coast, and by other natives who spent their winters inland on the Kobuk and Noatak rivers. It would seem that the Eskimos of Cape Prince of Wales, on the eastern side of Bering Strait, tried to set themselves up as middlemen, or to levy a toll on the traders as they passed by, just as the Trojans taxed the Greeks who visited or passed their city when trading in and out of the Black Sea. And just as the Greeks retaliated by besieging and sacking Troy, so the Siberians tried more than once to destroy the stronghold of their oppressors at Wales — if we may believe the traditions still current in that village, and trust the lookout shelters facing the strait that are visible on its hillside. As a rule, however, the Siberians avoided the proximity of Wales by crossing a little north of the strait, where they reduced the risk of discovery and could escape if detected. Then, shortly after the middle of the nineteenth century, some of the Wales natives took to buccaneering and began to raid the Eskimos of Kotzebue Sound; and about 1880, several boatloads of them even attacked the well-armed whaling ship of a Captain Gilly. A savage fight ensued, which Captain Cottle described to me as follows:

"The Eskimos came out in four or five umiaks, and the men, pretending that they wished to trade, left their women in the boats and swarmed on board the whaling ship. Suddenly one of them crept up behind the captain and stood poised to drive a knife into his back when a watchful sailor knocked him down with a handbar. The pirates immediately launched a general attack, but were quickly overcome by the ship's crew. Some jumped overboard and, pulling themselves into their umiaks, fled toward the shore; but Gilly opened fire on them and sank their whole flotilla. The rest tried to hide in the dark forecastle; these the sailors dragged out with a large hook, dispatched them, one by one, with a blow on the head, and threw their bodies into the sea. There was great rejoicing among the Kotzebue Eskimos when they heard that the pirates had been exterminated. As for the surviving population of Wales, it was too cowed by the disaster to give any further trouble."

Besides housing her own crew, the *Belvedere* housed also the crew of the ill-fated *Elvira*, who had abandoned that crippled schooner just before she disappeared in the storm. The half-hundred seamen consumed so many tons of provisions during the seven winter months that by the time April came around the *Belvedere* was considerably lighter than when she had been frozen in; and one midnight, after the warm sun of late April had loosened the grip of the ice around her sides, she suddenly broke free and leaped five feet into the air. Dishes clattered, spars fell crashing to the deck, and wild confusion reigned for a few minutes. But the near-panic soon subsided when the vessel regained her proper buoyancy and became once more immobile.

I walked down to Icy Reef with one of the *Belvedere*'s Siberian natives who had orders to deliver a sack of flour to an Eskimo family and to freight back on his empty sled a load of firewood. Icy Reef is a long sand bar separated from the mainland by a shallow lagoon, which in summer is a paradise for ducks and other waterfowl, but at this date was covered by a sheet of glare ice too slippery to venture upon. Three Eskimo families from the Mackenzie delta had pitched their rectangular cloth tents near the sand bar's western end, and while the women feverishly stitched water boots for the crew of the *Belvedere*, their husbands hunted ptarmigan, the only edible bird yet available to them — unless, indeed, they resorted to the snowy owls which, after several hours of boiling, might still be too tough for their consumption, though less refractory perhaps to their dogs. A slight current probably runs along the coast off Icy Reef, for the sea ice seems to break up there before it leaves Martin Point; and these Mackenzie natives

An Eskimo family

were awaiting that breakup in the hope of shooting some seals in the open water. One of them had already built a high staging from which to scan the horizon for a lead, and for any stray seals that might venture to sun themselves on the surface of the ice. But as yet no seals had appeared, and the three families were reduced to a very meager diet, nothing but baking-powder biscuits and whatever ptarmigan the men happened to bring in.

Hospitable as ever, despite the emptiness of their larder, they invited me to stay and share their baking-powder biscuits (that day even ptarmigan was lacking). I spent a pleasant hour with them, then continued alone down Icy Reef, searching for ancient ruins. Near its eastern end I met four more Mackenzie delta men and women who were making their way to the *Belvedere*; and not long afterward I waved a greeting to two sleds whose improvised sails, billowing before a fresh breeze, drove them along as fast as their owners could walk. Finally I reached the cabin at Demarcation Point, where McConnell was diligently typing a list of the stores, and the two biologists from the *Polar Bear* were absorbed in some specimens they had just brought in. I joined them in a very ample supper, then lay down in a corner for a few hours before wandering away to reconnoiter the neighborhood. Neither on this nor on other occasions did the bright sunlight disturb my rest, although my system seemed to need less sleep during this period of unbroken day.

Less than a mile from the cabin were the remains of what appeared to be the largest settlement between Barter Island and the Mackenzie River, some thirty log houses in all, a few with platforms or stagings beside them. None of them were old, however, perhaps not more than fifty or seventy years; although had I examined the ground after the melting of all the snow I might have discovered the outlines of earlier houses whose frames had completely rotted away. Tradition stated that the builders were Eskimos from the Mackenzie delta; but whether they lived in these huts the whole winter, or only in the late autumn, none of the natives whom I questioned seemed able to tell me. They did tell me, however, that during the midwinter months no lanes of water

Camp on Icy Reef

open up off Demarcation Point, as they do off Barrow and Point Barrow; so that fifty years before, when as yet no whalers had visited this coast and no traders had set up permanent depots, any Eskimos who remained here throughout the winter must have obtained their daily food by patiently watching over the breathing holes that seals maintain in the ice — an arduous method of hunting, remunerative only in localities where seals are unusually plentiful, which is not the case at Demarcation Point. It is true that herds of caribou found good summer grazing along the coastal plain on each side of the point, but in October or early November those animals invariably retreated to the shelter of the mountains. I suspect, therefore, that the settlement here was a summer trading rendezvous like Barter Island, that the eastern traders moved from their tents into the log cabins about the time of the freeze-up, but that as soon as the caribou disappeared into the mountains they too abandoned the locality and retired to winter homes in the Mackenzie delta.

Time may confirm or disprove this supposition. In any case, there can be little doubt that in the middle of the nineteenth century the traffic between the Siberian and Kotzebue Sound natives, and the penetration of white exploring vessels beyond Bering Strait, produced great unrest all along the Arctic coast as far east as the Mackenzie delta. From Kotzebue Sound trade followed the Kobuk and Noatak rivers to the head of the Colville River, whence the forbears of Arlook and Arksiatark carried it to the

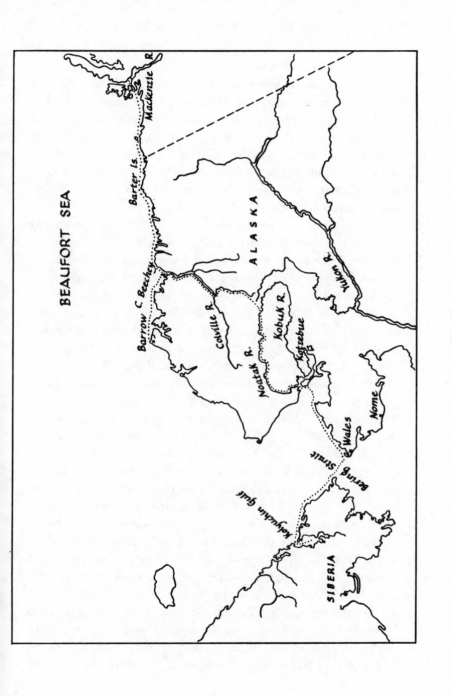

Beaufort Sea. Stefansson was told that the Colville River natives met the Barrow Eskimos at Cape Beechey, and that the Barrow natives, when the trading ended, left their women at the cape and sailed eastward to trade with Mackenzie River people at Collinson Point, Barter Island, or some other place not far west of the international boundary. A very old Mackenzie native confirmed Stefansson's report, and added that the women remained behind, not for convenience but for safety. Even he could remember how the trading had sometimes terminated in bloody quarrels that spared neither age nor sex.

A little of the turmoil died away about 1890, when the whalers began to enter the Beaufort Sea and not only called at Herschel Island near the mouth of Mackenzie River, but even wintered in its tiny harbor. Thereafter the Eskimos of that area no longer needed to travel westward in order to buy from the Barrow natives — for double and treble their legitimate price — guns, knives, and other desirable goods of white manufacture. The whalers now brought these goods right to their doors. Unhappily they brought at the same time less desirable things that had been equally unknown before, diseases such as measles, influenza, and syphilis that carried the Eskimos off like flies, since they had never developed the slightest immunity to them. From the whalers, too, the natives learned to make a potent rum by evaporating molasses in a primitive still — just two kerosene tins, one set over a fire and the other imbedded in snow, connected by a pipeline also fashioned from kerosene tins. The grog deranged their wits, the more so because they had not tasted alcoholic liquor before; and in their madness they stabbed and shot each other until, between diseases and murders, they had reduced their numbers to less than one fifth of the pre-European total. Similar excesses occurred at Barrow and Point Barrow, where the population suffered a corresponding decline. But then the Nunatarmiut or inland Eskimos between that point and the Mackenzie delta, who had hitherto fished and hunted caribou in the mountains during the winter months in place of hunting seals along the coast, moved eastward and westward out of their fastnesses to replenish the ranks of their nearly exterminated neighbors. By 1914 half or more of the Eskimos around Barrow and Point Barrow were of "foreign" extraction; and twenty years later not more than fifteen Mackenzie natives could claim descent from the original population. Even the dialect of the latter region underwent a change, for certain sounds and grammatical forms used by the Mackenzie natives whom I encountered differed from those recorded fifty years earlier by the French missionary Petitot, but coincided or nearly coincided with the sounds and forms I had learned at Barrow.

After wandering for a day among the ruins at Demarcation Point, I deposited my sleeping bag on the sled of a passing Eskimo and returned to the *Belvedere*, where another sled was preparing to leave for Camden Bay. Two officers of the ill-starred *Elvira,* the engineer and the assistant engineer, walked with me from the *Belvedere* to the *Polar Bear* camp. They were tall, heavily built men in their fifties, typical sourdoughs who had spent almost their whole lives in Alaska and tried their luck at every conceivable occupation. The engineer had just lost his whole fortune with the vanishing of the *Elvira*, of which he had been part owner. Years before, he had staked another fortune in a sea-otter enterprise: he had equipped a dozen or more Aleutian islanders with Winchester rifles and sent them out in their two-holed and three-holed kayaks to shoot the otters in the open waters of the Gulf of Alaska. The venture might have brought him rich profits three

Ruins at Demarcation Point

decades earlier, but by his day the animals had become so rare that he barely made good the expenses of his operation, even with the pelts bringing in from $500 to $3000 apiece according to their size and quality. Excessive hunting over a period of a hundred years had nearly destroyed the species; and it was but a short time after he wound up his operations that the United States government imposed a rigid ban on the hunting of sea otters to save them from total extinction.

Equally colorful had been the career of the assistant engineer. During four successive summers between 1880 and 1890 he had participated in the hunting of fur seals on the Pribiloff Islands, an activity open at that period to all comers, but regulated today by an international agreement between the United States, Canada, Japan, and the Soviet Union. In one season alone, he said, he and his fellow hunters killed 15,000 seals, all of them young males who, unable to find mates, went inland to drowse and slumber during the warm nights of the long summer, while the old males and the females slept with their young in rookeries nearer the sea. The hunters herded the young males like sheep to the slaughtering ground, cut out those that were ready for killing, a score or more at a time, and butchered them one by one by striking them on the head with a hard club, after which they drove the immature animals into the sea to become their victims a year later.

Both the engineer and the assistant engineer had panned for gold in Alaska's gravels; both had traded in furs and themselves trapped the fur-bearing animals. Although they appeared strong and vigorous still, a heaviness in their walk betrayed how hardships and the years were beginning to weigh on them. The Arctic is no place for single men who have passed their prime. One may hope that these two old-timers returned to the United States as soon as summer came, and in the milder climate of their own land spent their declining years in comfort.

Northern Alaska at this period was dotted with such frontiersmen — pioneers of civilization, or derelicts of it, according to one's personal viewpoint. The majority had come direct from the United States, but they counted in their ranks men of various nationalities, including some Scandinavians, a Belgian, a French-Canadian, and even a wanderer from Japan. I imagine that Billy Natkusiak, Stefansson's Eskimo companion, belonged to the same restless breed, for it exists in every race, whatever its color and cultural level. In north Alaska some of the men stayed for a few years only, with or without the company of native women; but others, for instance Brower and Brick's father, took to themselves Eskimo wives, raised families, and established permanent homes. A few of their half-breed descendants still retained one foot in the world of whites, and provided the territory with its best hope for the future, because they lived the same life as the Eskimos, used the Eskimo tongue as their own, and could interpret our white civilization to their kin better than could any outsiders.

My two old-timers dropped out at the *Polar Bear* camp, and I continued the journey with a younger man, a stocky Russian in his early twenties who had been the *Polar Bear*'s interpreter along the Siberian coast before the vessel rounded Point Barrow. This man too had inherited or acquired the spirit of the frontier, for in November, after his shipmates were comfortably installed in winter quarters, he had detached himself from them and built a small cabin six miles away. There, alone, he remained all winter, tending a few fox traps and avoiding the main camp except when he needed fresh supplies. One night noises outside his cabin disturbed him, and in the morning he found it ringed with polar-bear tracks; but his nocturnal visitor, satisfied with the one inspection, did not molest him further. Although only four foxes rewarded his exertions he was well satisfied, considering them net profit which he would not have gained had he hibernated with his shipmates. However, now that spring had come, he was dismantling the cabin and rejoining his vessel so that he could assist in its overhaul before the ice broke up.

When we reached the cabin he made tea on his primus, and shared with me the bread-and-butter sandwiches we had brought with us. Discovering some "mush," or corn-meal porridge, in a lard tin behind the stove he heated that too and divided it with me. Then we parted; he returned to the *Polar Bear* camp dragging all his possessions behind him, while I went on to Martin Point, there to await the sled party that was bringing my sleeping bag from the *Belvedere*.

All this day — it was May 5 — the snow was soft and slushy, for the weather had suddenly become quite warm. Snow buntings twittered round about, and new patches of brown earth appeared and expanded almost visibly. At Martin Point two snow-walled huts that had been roofed with canvas and occupied until a few days before were fast melting into the earth; one family had moved away altogether, the other, a Mackenzie Eskimo man and his mother, had transferred themselves to an ordinary tent pitched on bare ground a few yards distant. Martin Point, however, marked a kind of thermal boundary, because farther on, as I discovered the next morning, spring still lagged and the snow was distinctly firmer.

Ever since leaving Demarcation Point I had been pressing on the heels of an elderly Mackenzie native named Stone, who was traveling westward with his wife to spend a part of the summer with his old friend Ayacook. I overtook them at Martin Point. The following morning they allowed me to place my sleeping bag on their sled, which carried very little except their own bed skins, a tent, and a large seal poke filled with blubber. Together we slowly tramped ten miles to the empty cabin of a Danish trapper who had abandoned his trap line shortly after Christmas to take service with Stefansson. There we boiled some tea and after resting for perhaps an hour, pushed on, arriving about 8:30 P.M. at Arey Island, where Ayacook's tent had now been joined by Terigloo's. Both men were away hunting ptarmigan and marmots, but Mrs. Terigloo set before me a cold boiled ptarmigan and some biscuits, while Mrs. Ayacook entertained my companions, the Stones. The latter, who had now reached the end of their journey, unloaded their sled after supper and pitched their tent beside Ayacook's, while I stretched myself out in Terigloo's tent and slept.

Before midnight I awoke and, feeling greatly refreshed, set out

The Ayacooks

alone for our base in Camden Bay. It was moderately light, with the sun not far below the horizon; but the atmosphere was a little foggy, and the sled trails obliterated in many places by the mild weather. I knew, however, that my course lay a little south of west, and I trusted my two guides, a light breeze behind me and the faint glow of the sun as it moved from northwest around to northeast. The latter failed me soon after I started, because the fog became denser and the glow no longer visible; but all went well for nearly five hours, when I discovered that I was walking over tundra. I veered to the northwest; there too my knife struck tundra under the snow. I swung due north, and in a few minutes stumbled among rough ice hummocks that certainly lay seaward of the trail. Puzzled, I turned west again, and when the rough ice continued swerved southwest and finally south. Suddenly the fog lifted a little, and the sun, piercing half through, revealed a cache barely fifty yards to my left, a cache that I knew stood on Anderson Point, the eastern boundary of Camden Bay. My course from here was clear. Indeed, just beyond the cache, I came upon a well-marked trail that led me without interruption to our base.

IN THE Arctic as elsewhere nature's ways are hard to understand. Why was it, for example, that from Demarcation Point westward spring — the full spring, I mean, not just its first whispers — had followed after me, when logic seemed to indicate that it should have gone before. As soon as I passed Martin Point the snow became surprisingly harder, and the patches of bare ground less numerous; and whereas the flocks of ptarmigan that had been abundant around Arey Island during the preceding two weeks were already dispersing in search of new feeding grounds, and a few marmots were emerging from their holes to be caught in Terigloo's snares, at Camden Bay not a single marmot had been seen above ground and the ptarmigan were only just arriving.

Clearly spring had lingered. But it did not tarry long. In mid-May, just a week after my return to the base, we felt the first raindrops, and afterward the temperature, although it still averaged below freezing, began to rise steadily, causing considerable ground fog during the next few days as more and more brown earth soaked in the warmth of the midday sun.

Then came May 25. At 10 A.M. the thermometer reached 42° F. and held that level until evening, when it dropped to 32° F., just low enough to permit a light snowfall. Water began to flow everywhere: at our base three men dug trenches all day to divert the torrents from the cabin and tents. New birds suddenly appeared. Wandering inland I disturbed a flock of snipe that were feeding on the bare tundra; then eight seagulls flew over my head, and soon afterward a snowy owl with plumage already half black. At evening on the same day I sighted a skua gull, and later a flock of brant. That night the rivers broke out all along the coast; their roar could be heard twenty miles away, and their dark waters, newly exposed to the light, reflected their somberness in the sky above. Spring had reached us at last.

Although the birds were returning, the insects still delayed their coming. Yet they too would arrive within two or three weeks, and it was wise to prepare for them. Jennie Thompson made me a butterfly net, since I had promised our zoologist to capture some moths and butterflies for his collection. Being a man first, however, and a scientist second, I reflected that it was more important to obtain some protection against the mosquitoes that would soon hatch from every swamp and pool, and with that purpose in mind sought counsel of another lady who was riper in years than Jennie, and more richly stored with hard experience. Between us we devised a new model of Stetson that would support a veil. My collaborator cut two rings from the stiff hide of a bearded seal, stitched them together at right angles to form a brim and a band, and covered them with brown denim outside and with pink cotton within. The crown thus consisted of two layers of cloth separated by an airspace through which no mosquito could possibly reach my head. In one further burst of inventiveness she perforated the front of the veil with a tiny buttonhole through which I could pass my pipe. Had she seen me later calmly puffing smoke into the clouds of mosquitoes that buzzed around my face, she would have exulted as much as I did that our human intelligence had triumphed so gloriously over the insect's proboscis. Her Stetson served me faithfully for two and a half summers, after which I bequeathed it to an Eskimo companion who had long viewed it with covetous eyes.

My milliner was not a Mackenzie Eskimo woman, but a Nuna-tarmiut or inlander who, with sixty or seventy others, had just moved down from the Brooks range by way of the Hulahula River. (The word *Hulahula*, "dance," is not Eskimo but Polynesian. Perhaps Hawaiian Islanders from a whaling vessel had attended an Eskimo dance at the mouth of the river.) These inlanders were well acquainted with our part of the coast, for in the previous autumn they had cached three umiaks and a kayak on stagings so near our base that we could see them from the cabin. One couple with the unusually large number of five children had actually been camping on the shore of the bay when the *Mary Sachs* arrived, and, at some sacrifice to themselves, had traded half a sack of sugar to that schooner, whose whole supply had been loaded by mistake on the *Alaska*. Now, nine months later, they recalled the friendly contact, and, leaving their companions a day's journey up the Hulahula, traveled ahead to our base, where we entertained them at supper before they unloaded their sled to set up their tent.

An inlander's camp

The main body of the inlanders arrived the next day, a caravan of thirteen sleds piled high with caribou skins, one sled alone carrying nearly a hundred. Men and women together leisurely unlashed the sleds and deposited their loads on the bare ground, placing to one side the long willow sticks that they needed for the frameworks of their tents. They planted these sticks in a circle and lashed together their tips, just as Mrs. Arksiatark had lashed hers in midwinter; then they roofed the conical frame, not with canvas as she had done, but with caribou hides, employing five for some tents, six for others. Only above the doorway did they substitute a piece of cloth, inset with a rectangular window stitched from seal intestines and pierced with a round hole for a stovepipe. The hide of a grizzly gave them a satisfactory door; hanging free, it admitted a certain amount of fresh air, but no one objected to drafts at this season. Most of the tents were floored with brushwood to keep the bed skins from touching the damp ground; those that lacked brushwood made shift with strips of canvas.

In their dress the inlanders resembled all other Eskimos in Arctic Alaska; they wore a parka and trousers of caribou fur, and boots with uppers of either seal or caribou fur and soles of sealskin. Over the fur parka most of them pulled a windbreaker of cloth, cut to exactly the same pattern. The young women seemed to be as fond of silver rings as their cousins around Barrow; one of the unmarried girls flaunted no fewer than four. Only three elderly men still retained the tonsure of earlier days; the others, here as elsewhere, clipped their hair evenly over the whole head. Both sexes were inclined to hold the mouth agape, a habit that may be common to most Eskimos, since I noticed it farther west, and also among the Mackenzie delta natives; probably it arises from the difficulty of breathing when the temperature is low and the humidity high. Generally speaking, I could see little in the appearance or manners of these inland natives to mark them off from their Barrow kin except the shape of their tents, their use of sleds with higher runners than was any longer fashionable at Barrow, and, less certainly, a greater percentage of persons of Arksiatark's build, that is to say, taller and less stocky than the average coast native, and with long and rather narrow faces. Distinct from all the rest was a youngish man whose complexion was a coppery bronze. His nominal father was an Eskimo, but I think his real father must have been a Polynesian sailor from a whaling ship.

When the caravan arrived in Camden Bay one of the sleds bore a middle-aged woman who was so ill that her relatives had to carry her inside her tent. Four days later Jennie, who credited me with remarkable skill as a doctor because I had recently filled a cavity in one of her front teeth, begged me to visit the invalid and give her some medicine, since she had been unable to eat for several days. I found the patient sinking fast: at times her pulse almost stopped beating, and she was lapsing into a coma. Merely as a gesture, for I knew that it was useless, I directed that some hot broth be sent over to her tent; but she died the next morning, leaving a husband and two daughters, one of them still unmarried.

The Eskimos held the funeral service twelve hours afterward. They enclosed the body in a wooden coffin, set it on the ground in front of the tent, and, gathering around, the men with uncovered heads, sang in their own tongue a few Christian hymns. Then a young man produced a well-thumbed notebook and read from it a short prayer that had been translated into the Mackenzie Eskimo dialect by the Reverend (later Archdeacon) Whittaker, an Anglican missionary stationed in the Mackenzie delta. The men covered their heads again, someone passed around two plates filled with small slices of caribou fat, one slice for each person, and the coffin was then deposited on top of a cached umiak, where it would be safe from the dogs until such time as it could be transported to an old burial ground on Flaxman Island. There the ceremony ended. Outwardly at least it had been conducted with as much sincerity and reverence as any Christian funeral. Only at its close did I observe one surviving superstition; the widower, dismantling his tent, re-erected it twenty yards away so that the shade of the dead woman might not trouble her bereaved family.

Her death did not impair my reputation as a doctor, apparently, because a week later a man came to our cabin, and, after presenting me with some meat from a polar bear he had recently shot, asked me to cure his young daughter, whose mouth was so sore that she could not eat. I dared not refuse him, much as I realized my ignorance of things medical, lest he should believe me unfriendly and even accuse me of bewitching his child; so I hastily put together a few medicines and accompanied him to his tent, which was pitched on a sand bar nine miles to the westward. To my surprise the daughter proved to be a year-old baby who was suffering from ulcers on the lips and inside the mouth. I washed them as best I could with a mild solution of potassium permanganate, which, if not beneficial, could do them no harm, and promised the father that I would return after two days. But during my absence mother nature took over the case and herself healed most of the sores, so that by the time I paid my next visit the child was eating normally again. As always, however, mother nature insisted on remaining anonymous, and it was I who, undeservedly, received all the credit.

The natives had brought on their sleds only a small supply of meat, the residue of the caribou and sheep they had killed in the mountains. A few men went northward each morning to stalk any seals that might be basking on the surface of the ice; but in ten days they sighted and killed only one, because the weather was too cold to lure the animals out of their breathing holes. Meanwhile the majority of the hunters combed the land for ptarmigan, which suddenly swarmed around us for a fortnight before dispersing to build their nests. Each evening they brought in at least three dozen birds. But even that number could not satisfy the hunger of half a hundred people, and a famine seemed imminent unless the weather quickly improved.

There was a young married woman in the band who armed herself with a double-barreled shotgun and marched inland with the ptarmigan hunters as often as her husband scoured the ice for seals. I saw her return one evening with two birds, but could not discover whether in general she was more successful, or less successful, than her companions. I did learn, however, that both she and a second young woman not only shot ptarmigan and other birds, but frequently joined the men in their caribou hunts and even went out alone to stalk seals. The Eskimos seemed to consider this quite natural — as indeed it was; for not every young woman, strong and active and still childless, could contentedly spend her days in a cabin or tent dressing skins, making and mending the clothing, cooking one or at the most two meals a day, and idling away the remaining hours in gossip with her neighbors.

Nearly all the inlanders used Winchester rifles of 30.30 or .44 gauge. The 30.30 was the more powerful weapon, but several hunters preferred the .44 because for that gauge, and for that alone, they could buy powder, caps, lead, and the simple hand tools necessary for reloading the brass cartridges. Lead bullets they could cast without difficulty by fusing the metal in a small frying pan over a primus stove and pouring the molten liquid into the mold that accompanied the reloading outfit. In fact, it was so easy for them to reload their .44 rifle shells, and also the brass shells of their shotguns, that one could almost condone the prodigality with which they expended their ammunition and their utter indifference to marksmanship.

On May 21, a scout reported that there was a lane of open water to the westward, whereupon the families folded up their tents and moved away, abandoning our base to its earlier solitude. Two delayed for a day so that they might renew their stock of ammunition by trading a few furs with our seamen. Since the only furs they showed us were those of the red fox and its varieties, black, silver-gray, and cross, I concluded that the white fox does not penetrate into the haunts of the red species on the southern slopes of the Brooks range, although the red species certainly crosses occasionally to the north side, for a local Eskimo had trapped one during the winter on the coast near Flaxman Island.

Hardly had the last of the inlanders moved away when Ayacook appeared to warn me that if I intended to dig up the ruins at Barter Island I should transfer myself to that locality without delay, because within a few days sled traveling might become impossible. That very night, indeed, the rivers broke their fetters and inundated miles of sea ice off their deltas, where their flooding waters gradually escaped through various cracks and crevices. There was no time to procrastinate. From Anderson, who had just returned from a trip to the Mackenzie delta, I secured official sanction for the arrangements I was making: that I would spend the next few weeks excavating around Barter Island; that our expedition would pay Ayacook $100 a month, and Ipanna, his elder stepson, $50 a month, for as long as they worked with me; that I would maintain contact with Camden Bay by means of Ayacook's umiak; and that I would either return to the bay before navigation reopened and our expedition sailed eastward, or would hold myself ready at Barter Island to embark on one or another of our schooners as they passed by. Having settled these and other details, I gathered together the tools and supplies I would need for excavating, loaded them on Ayacook's sled, and left with him for his camp.

The traveling was less difficult than we had anticipated, for even though we had to wade in water a foot or more deep, we were able to escape the main currents of the overflowing rivers by making wide detours. A week later we could probably have traveled part of the way by umiak, since already, after only a few hours of rampaging, the flood was widening the holes and expanding the cracks in the ice, which was about five feet thick in this area. Within another forty-eight hours, or at the most sixty, it would certainly cut long ribbons through it, ribbons that would grow and lengthen until they finally joined together and converted the sea into a maze of floating ice pans for a distance of two or three miles from shore. Ayacook had timed our departure none too soon.

We reached his camp at 5 A.M. Old Stone and his wife were still there, and also Terigloo and his family; the latter, however, quietly moved on to Barter Island toward evening. We and the Stones lingered a day so that Ayacook might sort out his property and store away everything that he would not need during the next five or six weeks. I helped him in this task, while his two stepsons,

Ayacook's cache

Ipanna and the younger boy Kovanna, went off to track down some geese and eider ducks that had flown over our heads and landed, they thought, somewhere in the vicinity.

The construction of Ayacook's cache presented no difficulty. We merely laid a few logs in a row on the bare ground, piled the surplus goods on top of them, covered them with three large canvases and weighted down the pile with other logs. There they would be safe throughout the summer, since no birds would touch them, and no marauding animals could reach the island until the freeze-up. One object only, a large polar-bear hide, he laid to one side, considering it too valuable to leave on the ground. Instead, he hoisted it to the top of a high pole firmly anchored with guy ropes, lest the dogs of some passing traveler should smell it out and, pouncing on it unobserved, tear it to shreds in a few seconds.

The boys failed to find the geese and the eider ducks, but we dined exceedingly well on mountain-sheep meat that Ayacook had obtained from an inlander. Twenty-four hours later we landed on the west end of Barter Island and pitched our tents near Terigloo's amid the ruins of fifteen houses, of which the last, more conspicuous and evidently more recent than the rest, still retained the conical framework of a kitchen. We even scratched the soil in two or three places, for I was impatient to begin excavating; but the ground was frozen and rock-like below the first inch. In any case it was too cold for us to dig steadily, chilled by temperatures that remained most of the time well below the freezing point. So cold was it that for four nights I lay shivering inside my tent when I should have been sleeping, having imprudently left my winter sleeping bag of caribou fur in Camden Bay and brought with me only a woolen bag inside a cover of burberry; no wind could penetrate the burberry, but a cold damp air seeped through it from all sides and chilled me to the bone. Not until I had made myself a tight-fitting coffin — lidless naturally — from the planks and logs of driftwood on the beach did I sleep in comfort again.

We could not excavate much yet, but neither could we afford to spend the days in idleness. While sled traveling was still possible I sent Ayacook's stepsons to Martin Point to bring back the provisions our expedition had stored there on the chance that they might be needed at some future date. Meanwhile we who remained behind hunted ptarmigan and whatever other game we could discover on the land, for we needed the fresh meat. Some ptarmigan, we noted on May 29, were already beginning to nest, since we found unlaid eggs inside their bodies.

Among our trophies were an owl and a lemming, both of which I skinned for the biological collections of the expedition. Mrs. Stone, who had killed the lemming with a stick, called the tiny creature *kilagmiutark*, "sky dweller," believing that it had come down from the sky during a snowstorm and, had she not killed it, would have changed later into a fox. At least that was the belief of her parents. They had set great value on the animal's white winter fur, which they attached to the back or front of the parka, or, occasionally, to an ornamental cap that they wore at dances.

More and more seals were now emerging from their breathing holes to bask in the warm sun, challenging each of us to keep a weather eye on the field of gray-white ice for any speck that seemed abnormally black. We sighted a seal the morning after we reached Barter Island, and Ayacook, making a wide circuit, approached within rifle range of it; but when he attempted to crawl a little closer in order to make sure that his bullet would register an instantaneous kill, the animal heard him and dived into its hole.

Seals possess a keen sense of hearing to compensate for their shortsightedness, and alert at the slightest noise that suggests the proximity of their inveterate enemy, the polar bear. On the other hand, they are prone to disregard low scratching sounds such as they themselves make when crawling over the ice. Ayacook, like other Eskimos, was aware of this, and kept a pair of seal claws for scratching the ice rhythmically in the same manner as his quarry. If the animal was unusually alert and gazed at him suspiciously, he either lay motionless until it dropped its head again, or he moved his own head slowly from side to side as if he too were a seal cautiously searching the horizon for possible enemies. Such tactics had been very necessary in his father's day, when the natives needed to creep within a dozen or fifteen yards of their victims before they dared launch their hand harpoons; but they became out-of-date from the moment the hunters obtained high-powered rifles that could drive a bullet through the brain of a seal a hundred yards away. If Ayacook revived them now and again, it was for precisely the same reason as some of our dilettante hunters betake themselves to the bow and arrow — pure sport.

Two more seals eluded him by diving into the water, but finally he shot a large male that provided us with meat for several days. A few hours later Terigloo, with no weapon except his hunting knife, dispatched a seal that he found wandering over the ice, vainly seeking a hole through which to re-enter the water. Its strange predicament astonished my companions, who concluded, after a long discussion in camp, that a slight movement in the ice field must have closed its breathing hole and marooned it while it was drowsing on the surface.

As I sat one morning in the doorway of Ayacook's tent, waiting until his wife had mended my boots and greased them with seal blubber, a whole regiment of old-squaw ducks flew swift and high toward us — six squadrons, one behind the other, each of about a dozen birds in line. Mrs. Ayacook shrieked *aharlik, aharlik,* echoing the birds' cry to draw them nearer the earth, while every man in the camp caught up his shotgun and fired furiously. Since even the nearest of the squadrons was far out of range, the cannonade merely diverted them ten or twenty degrees off their course and drove them to settle farther away.

Time after time my companions dissipated their cartridges in this manner; of every ten shots that they fired only about one ever found its mark. Not that it mattered greatly at this period, because they possessed ample supplies of powder, shot, and caps. But they seemed to harbor some psychological quirk which made them more careless and improvident of ammunition and other things that they acquired from the traders than of objects that pertained to their pre-European economy. It was a virus that infected all the Eskimos between Barrow and the Mackenzie delta. I had noticed another instance of it during the winter, when some of the Barrow trappers had used their primus stoves with needless prodigality as long as their kerosene lasted, and then had found themselves without kerosene just when they most needed it.

Aharlik, the old-squaw duck, was not the only bird with a name that reproduced its note. There was the delicate *liwaliwak,* Baird's sandpiper, that peeped *liwa liwa* as it pattered along the beach; and from the middle of some pond, or from high up in the sky, the *toodlik,* yellow-billed loon, would utter a long-drawn-out *too* like a train whistle and end with a sharp *dlik* four notes higher. The Eskimos loved to imitate these bird notes, as white children echo the call of the cuckoo and the whoo of the owl.

The days moved rapidly around to Sunday, which my companions, like the western natives, scrupulously observed as a day of rest. The hunters put away their rifles and shotguns, and gathered inside Stone's tent for a short service. There I left them and, taking my butterfly net, wandered over the island on a reconnoitering excursion.

The snow had now vanished from more than half the land, and

A loon

its melt-water had gathered into myriads of little ponds or was hurrying in countless rivulets toward the sea. Everywhere the frost of a thousand winters had heaved and hummocked the ground into spongy "niggerheads," overgrown with mosses and lichens and separated by soggy pools; and wherever the ground was too dry for niggerheads its surface was cracked in all directions as though a fire had raged underneath. Many of the cracks had provided ready-made channels for the running water, which had gullied them deeper and deeper until some had developed into genuine ravines. In these the snow still lingered, and the water either drained over it, or raced in tunnels beneath its surface. At one place I came upon an echoing waterfall where a stream that had cut a trench three feet deep in the snow filling of a ravine dropped suddenly six feet into a large pool ringed with perpendicular walls of snow, from which it spilled over into a narrow gorge. In another place water entered the earth through cracks at the bottom of a large hollow, and, after flowing underground for a short distance, broke out from its subterranean passage in a steadily flowing brooklet. Thus was nature scoring and eroding the island, although no part of it appeared to be more than thirty feet above sea level.

And there were still stranger phenomena. A surprising number of ponds were circular, filling deep, saucer-shaped depressions in the level ground that curiously resembled the dewponds left by prehistoric man on the chalk plateaus of southeast England. Only rarely did perceptible banks rim their niggerhead margins; yet no streams flowed from them, the water seeping from one pond to another through the surface soil. In certain places again, where the ground was more pebbly, I found "neolithic camps" in miniature, some round, some oval, within which nature seemed to have sorted out the pebbles according to their sizes. The commonest type had a central hummock—the "camp" proper—ringed by a tiny moat, and guarded in turn by a low rampart surrounded by a second moat; some camps, however, lacked the outer rampart and outer moat. Their dimensions varied greatly, but in one of the largest an inner moat 14 inches wide enclosed a camp that measured 5 feet long by 3½ feet wide. These strange formations doubtless owed their birth to the repeated freezing and thawing of the soil, but the exact mechanics of the process was beyond my comprehension.

Tundra of this nature did not make for easy tramping. Whatever direction I took, my course was bound to meander on account of the ponds and ravines. Progress was unimpeded and rapid as long as I kept to the patches of dry soil, whether they were barren or carpeted with ground-clinging dryads, oxytropi, and other plants; but such patches were few and scattered. To step from one quivering niggerhead to another required fine balancing and became in the end very fatiguing, but it was preferable to slipping or stepping between them into a soggy morass. Then too the snow-filled ravines had to be negotiated with caution. On another excursion a week later, having imprudently advanced upon an insignificant-looking ravine without first testing the strength of its snow cover, I suddenly found myself ankle-deep in its small stream, gazing upward at a distant sky through a circular hole five feet above my head.

Yet this wet Arctic tundra, exhausting though it might be to the traveler, teemed with interesting forms of life. There were no trees, of course, and no shrubs except a few low clumps of willow or alder growing in sheltered gulleys; but so abundant was the ground-clinging vegetation that the land resembled an uneven and much broken-up meadow. Only one plant had flowered at this date, the small pink silene; and no other blossomed until June 13, when the yellow ranunculus opened its buttercup-like petals. On that day we saw our first winged insects, some miserable bluebottles that buzzed around our unprotected food. Fortunately they did not become numerous until June 23, when the snow had vanished from all but the deeper ravines, baby sandpipers were running along the shore, and several more plants had begun to flower, among them the red thistle which my Eskimos sometimes plucked and sucked for its honey. The fragrance of this plant summoned the bumblebees, which suddenly emerged in numbers and murmured from flower to flower. Only two or three days later the mosquitoes marshaled their hosts, and they too hummed in ecstasy as they floated from man to man. By that time the earlier flowers were already fading, moths and butterflies had entered upon the scene, and summer, the brief Arctic summer, had unmistakably announced her arrival.

For the moment, however, summer was nearly a month away, and the butterfly net that I flourished as I rambled over the tundra might better have been left in my tent. To tell the truth, I was rather glad it was useless, and that I was not carrying a shotgun, because the world around me was very peaceful and serene, undisturbed by any noises except the occasional note of a bird and the silvery tinkle of running water. Here and there, to mark a trail or the location of a fox trap, someone had set on end black clods of turf that could be seen from two hundred yards; and a snarer of ptarmigan had omitted to dismantle a line of upright sticks still joined by the nooses he, or she, had stretched between them. I disturbed a snowy owl that was feeding on an old-squaw duck, probably one that my party had wounded; and near a few sled fragments I found a human skull half-buried in the moss, all that remained of some ancient grave. Doubtless the foxes and lemmings had made short shrift of it, the latter being so numerous on the island that I stumbled on at least six of their nests, which had been hidden in winter beneath the snow. A newcomer to the Arctic could easily have mistaken the little bunches of brown grass for deserted birds' nests that had been blown hither and yon by the wind; but the experienced Ayacook had definitely attributed them to lemmings.

Hunger and weariness finally drove me back to camp, after an absence of several hours. The women, meanwhile, had prepared us a banquet from the game our hunters had brought in the day before. First there was boiled loon, which looked and tasted like goose; then came ptarmigan stewed with rice, and last of all boiled duck. Accompanying each course was a generous supply of baking-powder biscuits, and steaming cups of both tea and cocoa. My appetite failed me for the last course, but as I retired to my tent I felt that the meal had been a triumphal ending to a very satisfactory day.

W HEN we landed on the western sandspit of Barter Island and began to set up our tents near one end of its line of ruins, Terigloo, who two days earlier had quietly erected his tent at the other end, sent word that he too intended to investigate this site, having dug the previous summer on nearby Arey Island. It was Ayacook who brought me this news, and he seemed as annoyed as I was, for we both knew that the man had not intended to camp on Barter Island, or even to summer in its vicinity, until he got wind of our plans. Yet we could not object, because the island was public domain and our rights to dig were no greater than his. We stipulated, however, that he should confine his activities to the five ruins nearest his tent, leaving the other ten or eleven for our attention, and to this he agreed.

Our excavations proceeded slowly for a time, because the thaw had touched only the first inch of surface soil, below which the ground was frozen to an undetermined depth. This frozen section we could have chipped away with pickaxes as one chips rock, but not without destroying as many specimens as we left undamaged.

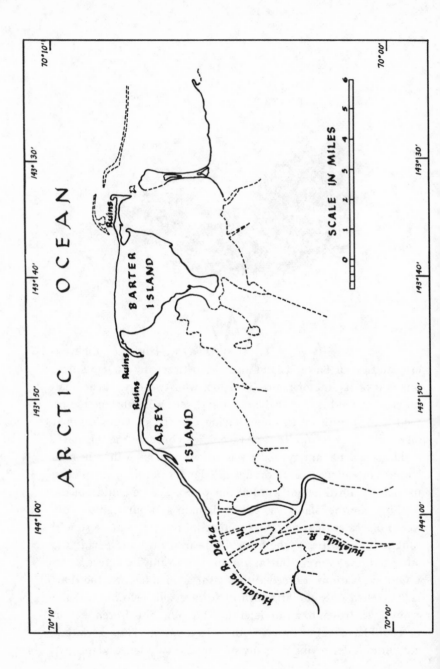

ARCTIC OCEAN

Ruins

Ruins   Ruins

AREY
ISLAND

BARTER
ISLAND

Hulahula R. Delta

Hulahula R.

SCALE IN MILES

0 1 2 3 4 5 6

Accordingly we stripped off the surface layer with shovels, waited two or three days until the new surface thawed an inch, and carefully peeled that away also with special scrapers made by bending over the ends of some flat files. A man could peel away an inch of a ruin's surface in about three hours, since no dwelling contained more than one room, or measured more than 240 square feet; the majority, indeed, covered only half that area. Their treasures, however, rested directly on the floor, and to reach that level the workman had to repeat the scraping at least twice, after intervals each time of three or more days. He could not possibly exhaust any particular house, therefore, in less than a week; but by working on three or four houses simultaneously, he could reduce the *average* time per house to a day and a half, which seemed fairly satisfactory. We tried to lower even that rate by kindling large fires on top of some ruins and thawing out their soil in a few hours; but we hastily abandoned the experiment when we discovered that the rapid change of temperature had cracked several of the stone and bone implements below the surface, among them a very fine harpoon-head of polished slate.

Early in June we extended our operations to the island's eastern sandspit, where the ruins were four times as numerous and apparently of greater antiquity. Within and alongside them protruded many whale skulls, which had been absent on the western sandspit; four lay at the head of one house, three at the head of another. The distance from our camp to this site was about four miles, whether we traveled over the tundra, or followed the shore line on the still-fast ice; generally we followed the tundra route, because it promised better duck shooting and more trophies for the evening pot. If the weather was mild we dug for about seven hours, with one short break for a hot dish of lima beans; but during the first half of June the temperature seldom rose more than six or eight degrees above the freezing point, and at times a cold breeze blowing off the sea ice so numbed our hands that we gladly dropped our tools after four or five hours only.

Back in camp Mrs. Ayacook prepared a substantial meal for us between 8 P.M. and 10 P.M. so that we might eat as soon as we re-

Whale skulls on Eskimo ruins

turned. Ayacook and Ipanna then went duck shooting again, or
they wandered out on the sea ice in search of seals, while I wrote
up the notes of the day's operations and skinned for our biological collections whatever birds we had shot. Our schedule was very
elastic, no one paying much attention to the exact time now that
the nights were as light as the days; but I tried to discourage too
intemperate hours, because lack of sleep was apt to sap the energy
of my workmen for the next digging shift, and Mrs. Ayacook regularly summoned us to breakfast about noon. Her husband caused
me no anxiety, for he was mature and unusually reliable; but we
could never quite depend on teen-aged Ipanna. Yet he too tried
to keep his restlessness within bounds, and worked so faithfully
that I refused to let his stepfather waken him when we found him
one day face downward on the floor of a ruin, still grasping his
iron scraper, but fast asleep.

From our first inspection of the eastern sandspit I had carried
back a human skull that was lying half-buried in the gravel of the
beach, and had deposited it without further thought in an open
box inside my tent. Ten days later, when we were returning from
work, Mrs. Ayacook intercepted us on the outskirts of camp to
register a grave complaint. She had been sewing inside her tent,
she said, when my tent a few paces away suddenly began to shake,
although the air was still; and right afterward her own tent too

shook so violently that she expected it to collapse on her head. Obviously the spirit owner of the skull that I was harboring in my tent was plotting mischief, and it was incumbent on me to do something about it.

She looked at me expectantly. I am a slow thinker and did not know what to answer. Then Ayacook came to my rescue.

"Nail a lid on the box," he said. "That will prevent it from doing us any harm."

Gratefully I promised to nail up the box that very evening; and his wife heaved a sigh of relief. Her shrewd husband did not tell her that the sack which I was carrying in my hand at that moment contained two more skulls which we had just unearthed on the eastern sandspit; and I hid them very carefully from her sight.

In our walks over the tundra each day we frequently startled a nestling sparrow, a longspur, or other small bird too insignificant to merit a place in our cooking pot. My companions always noticed them, as they noticed everything that moved; but as a rule they passed indifferently on. One day, however, Ayacook's younger stepson Kovanna, who was about twelve years old, lingered behind to set a noose over some eggs that a longspur had deserted at our approach. After arranging the snare to his satisfaction he lay on the ground a few yards away to await the mother bird's return; but the bird was cautious and kept out of sight. At last he lost patience, abandoned his snare and came running after us. I asked him, teasingly, in the words of a children's song that I had heard during the winter, whether he had "destroyed the nest and crushed the unhatched chicks"; but he only frowned a rather shamefaced no and said nothing. His brother Ipanna answered for him: "Kovanna isn't a child any longer, but a serious hunter like ourselves."

This boy Kovanna nearly always crossed with us to the eastern sandspit, where he spent most of his time shooting at birds with his brother's shotgun, or else with a bow and arrows that Ayacook had made for him. Our neighbor Terigloo also hunted all day, while the aging Stone, too feeble now to spend long hours at the chase, fossicked in our section of the ruins beside the camp, although we had ransacked them all, except the three end ones, whose floors were exposed but not yet thawed out. Mrs. Stone often fossicked with him, for she shared his nostalgia at the sight of weapons and household things which had been familiar to their childhood, but had then passed out of use. Together the old couple ferreted out all the secret corners and hiding places, and, with an instinct that seemed almost uncanny, brought to light a considerable number of objects that we had overlooked. Stone would bring them to my tent in the evening and hand them to me with a satisfied smile. At no time did he ask or seem to expect any payment; and I offered him none, but accepted his gifts as graciously as I could and reciprocated them whenever the opportunity presented itself.

One morning the old man was laid low by a violent stomach attack, and all the Eskimos gathered inside his tent to sing hymns and to pray for his recovery. The next day, when his condition showed no improvement, they held a second service; and when that too produced no result they asked me whether I could provide a remedy. I promised to try, remembering that among the half-dozen medicines I had brought from Camden Bay was a small supply of epsom salts. I administered an adequate dose of that cathartic, and followed it up twelve hours later with a teaspoonful of very thin paste made by mixing some flour with cold water — a remedy I had learned several years before from a veteran of the South African war, who declared that it had cured many soldiers of dysentery. It may or may not have been as effective in that campaign as he claimed, but in Stone's case at least it worked.

It was Stone's tent that the Eskimos always chose for the divine service they held each Sunday, a day, parenthetically, that was not our twenty-four-hour interval from one midnight to the next, but a somewhat indefinite period marked by the passage of the sun from east through south to west. As long as it was performing that half circle my companions would neither fire a shot nor throw a stone, even if a goose or an eider duck settled imprudently near their tents. But the moment the sun reached what they judged to be a western declination they seized their weapons

Mapterark

and hurried off, some over the ice to look for seals, others inland in quest of waterfowl; and they compensated for their previous abstinence by indulging in an orgy of shooting that echoed over the whole countryside. Their ardor burned itself out toward midnight, when one by one, they drifted back to camp and devoted the next two or three hours to some outdoor pastime like distance jumping, or sat on the floor of a tent and played poker.

Pools of water were now beginning to form along the shore, and many cracks in the ice to seaward. The sledding season was nearly over, but before it ended there arrived from the west an inland Eskimo named Mapterark, with his wife and two small children. Ayacook, their friend of many years' standing, welcomed them warmly and celebrated their arrival with a banquet to which every housewife in the camp inevitably contributed something. Mrs. Mapterark brought a pot of boiled duck, Mrs. Stone a kettle of tea, Mrs. Terigloo some sour-dough bread and a second kettle of tea, while our hostess, Mrs. Ayacook, produced boiled rice, baking-powder biscuits, and, of course, still more tea. The women formed a little circle of their own at this party, doubtless to discuss their sewing and other matters of little importance to the men.

Mapterark was a tall, athletic man, quiet in voice and manner but very active. The sealing around Camden Bay had proved so unrewarding, he told us, that the inlanders had been forced to scatter, and when the others moved westward, he took the opposite direction in order to try his luck at Barter Island. During his first fortnight with us he shot a number of waterfowl, but only four seals, possibly because the cool and at times foggy weather discouraged the animals from crawling out onto the surface of the ice; but in the second half of June his luck changed, and not a day went by in which he did not bring home at least one seal. On the 23rd he dragged back six, and three days later four — he was an excellent hunter.

I heard one midnight the sound of chanting, and going outside my tent, observed Mapterark's children gazing out from a low bank over the white ice plain where their father, a mile or more

Dragging home a seal

away, was dragging home another dead seal. Mrs. Mapterark hastily harnessed two dogs and led them out to help him, while the children, jumping up and down, repeated their chant:

"From the sea he is dragging something,
He, the sealer, who is returning home."

Barrow children had chanted a similar song when their parents returned successful from the sealing grounds. These Hyperboreans could not weave crowns of bay leaves for the victors, but at least they honored them with traditional hymns of praise.

Mid-June brought us to the pleasantest season of the year, when night had merged into day, the temperature was ideal for hunting, waterfowl abounded, and seals became every day more plentiful. My companions could live on the fat of the land and of the sea, with no thought for the morrow, since the hard days of the past winter had faded into memory and the next winter was three months ahead. Lightheartedly, then, they joked with each other and played games whenever they happened to be in camp together. Even the quiet Mapterark enjoyed striking small sparks from his companions.

"How old you are becoming," he quipped at Ipanna. "The girls don't seem to like you. I'm afraid you'll never find a wife now."

And the harassed youth bludgeoned back:

"What a pity that a good hunter like you should have such a monstrously long nose."

Staid Ayacook came in for his share of the banter. Once Terigloo's elder boy ran by us when we were descending a small gulley.

"Ayacook's an old man," he shouted.

Ayacook sped after him like a wolf, and, seizing him by the arm, dragged him panting up the opposite slope, where both man and boy fell to the ground exhausted.

So, literally and figuratively, our little community of four families basked contentedly in the late spring sunshine. Only one person, Terigloo, held himself a trifle aloof, shadowed as it were by a light cloud. His children played unrestrainedly with the other children, and his stoutish wife sewed and gossiped very placidly in our midst; but whenever he himself joined our company he seemed to wear the embarrassed air of a visitor who is not entirely sure of his welcome. I may have misjudged him, however, since I could not wholly suppress a slight resentment at having to share one of our archaeological sites with him, nor forget that he had been branded by the geologist Leffingwell as the only Eskimo along the coast who seemed incapable of feeling gratitude. Leffingwell's judgment had certainly been unduly harsh; for a week after Mrs. Terigloo had sought my help in extracting the end of a needle that had broken off in her palm, her husband laid at my door a pair of rare green-winged teal that he had found nesting in our vicinity, and departed quietly before I could even thank him.

Fortune seemed to reserve a special smile for Terigloo. After he dug intermittently for three weeks in the ruins we had allotted him beside our camp, and uncovered very little in the first ruin, he struck in the second a veritable gold mine. There some low earth walls less than a foot high, and two corner stumps that had rotted to ground level, sketched the outlines of a dwelling similar in plan and dimensions to the rude cabin I had helped Mrs. Arksiatark to build in Harrison Bay at Christmas. Nothing in its appearance suggested the unusual; it seemed just another ancient house that had been abandoned to the elements when its inmates moved away to another locality, taking with them all their possessions. But in this case the inmates had not moved away, and their possessions were all here in their places, for when Terigloo and his family had scraped away the decomposed fragments of the log roof and the turf that had covered it, they saw the stone lamp resting in its customary position close to the front wall, and on either side of it, with their heads so close that they seemed to be still seeking its long-vanished warmth, two skeletons, one male and the other female. Near the man was his bow, intact except for its sinew lashings; beside the woman her tubular needle-case still protecting in its hollow interior four needles, three of copper and one of jade; and strewn about the floor were flint and iron pyrites ready to strike a spark, knives, arrows, harpoon heads with flint blades, and numerous other objects, among them a large crystal of clear quartz which, in spite of its supposedly magical properties, had failed to stave off disaster. What had happened? Had husband and wife starved to death? Had some fatal disease smitten both simultaneously? Or had they sealed up their home so tightly against the bitter cold without that they perished from monoxide poisoning? No one will ever know.

Terigloo's unexpected discovery made my archaeological eyes bulge with envy. Not knowing what he might find in his remaining three houses, I promptly purchased all the specimens he had garnered already and took him into my service for two weeks at the same wage as Ayacook.

The days winged swiftly by. Already June was singing her last lines before surrendering the stage to summer. On our island the snow had melted everywhere except from the bottoms of some deep ravines. As I looked northward from the doorway of my tent I could see the thin lane of water along the beach's edge grow wider day by day, gradually breaking the ocean's icy grip upon the land. To the south, between our camp and the mainland, stretched a mile-wide lagoon of open water, half-encircled by our curving sandspit and tangented on the far side by the mile-high mountains. The tranquil sheen of this inlet magnified the few white ice pans that drifted over it, and doubled the number of ducks and geese that flew above. Once dark shadows rippled its surface as a flock of Pacific eiders, their brown bodies black against the pale blue sky, swept across the neck of our sandspit and continued eastward, infallible warning, so Ayacook informed me, of an approaching southwest wind. On the beaches and tundra every species of bird was nesting, or else shepherding its already hatched young. A timid snow bunting, raising perhaps a second brood, deposited its eggs in the deep safe hollow of a whale's skull that centuries before a long-forgotten Eskimo had dragged to the entrance of his home. We killed a white goose that had pecked the feathers from its breast to line its nest; and later, over the lagoon, Kovanna shot down a sea gull that carried a similar bare patch on its front, visible proof of its parental love. The boy retrieved this gull by bestriding a small ice pan and punting it over the water with a spare tent pole. We expected to see his precarious craft upend or break in two, but it served him more faithfully than another craft which he and Terigloo's elder boy constructed from driftwood; for the lashing of the more pretentious vessel gave way when it was fifty yards from land, and the two boys, precipitated into the shallow but ice-cold water, had to fight grimly over its oozy bed to reach the shore again.

While it was still possible to walk across the narrow strait that separated us from Arey Island, Ayacook and I re-examined that sand bar's numerous ruins, many of which had been ransacked previously by Terigloo and other curio-seekers. Then and there we agreed that he and his wife should dig into them for a few days, while Ipanna and I, with Terigloo's help, continued the excavations on the eastern sandspit of Barter Island. This arrangement pleased him greatly, because it gave him access to a virgin sealing ground; and it fitted in well with my own plans, since I needed specimens from this and other places to compare with our growing collections from Barter Island. He moved to the new location the same day, and twenty-four hours later, when I sighted through my binoculars a dark object hanging beside his white tent, I rejoiced that his hope of a successful seal hunt had been so quickly fulfilled.

Meanwhile, on one of his sealing excursions, Mapterark had noticed a few whitefish swimming in a large tide crack not far from shore; and he reported the discovery as soon as he arrived home. Mrs. Stone immediately hurried off to the crack with a fishing line, for this was one food-gathering activity in which even an old woman could be as successful as a man in his prime. But the whitefish were not biting on this occasion, or on another when she tried her luck. It could not have been the fault of her tackle, because that had been specially designed by her husband to tempt the most suspicious fish. He had carved its ivory lure, which was also its sinker, into the shape of a delicate fish, and inset dark pegs of iron to represent the fins and brighter pegs of brass the eyes. Then he had riveted through its mouth an iron nail, bent and sharply pointed, but barbless, since a fisherman skilled in jigging requires no barb; and from the root of this hook he had strung a short ribbon of red flannel backed by white seal-skin which, like a fish, changed shape and color as it trailed through the water. For all its allure, however, his bait failed to attract the whitefish, although a week later, when the tide crack had expanded into a wide lane of water stretching from the pack ice to the shore, more than a score became enmeshed in two nets that had been set by Mapterark and Terigloo.

With the opening of July we confidently expected summer weather, but during the first ten days of that month the sky remained generally overcast, the thermometer refused to ascend higher than 43° F., and cold winds accompanied by rain and even snow slackened the pace of our excavations. Nevertheless, the surface of the ground continued its slow thaw, more and more butterflies fluttered around us, and the ice to seaward began to break up so fast that Mapterark hurriedly overhauled the lashings of his kayak and greased its seams with seal oil. By July 2 the lagoon at our back was lapping the shore of Arey Island and peering into Ayacook's tent. He and his wife, unable to resist its invitation, launched their umiak and crossed over to visit us. After rendering an account of their digging they agreed to close down their work and rejoin us, so that our entire party might concentrate on the eastern sandspit of Barter Island, where the ruins seemed older and more numerous. Refreshed then by a light meal and copious cups of tea, they sailed back to Arey Island, taking with them Terigloo, who wanted to bring over his own umiak, cached there since the previous autumn.

Before they returned Ipanna and I explored the sea lanes around Barter Island. Although open water now fringed the shore on both sides of our camp, the pack ice still maintained its grip along the north coast of the island and effectually barred our passage eastward by that route. Behind us, however, the lagoon that divided us from the mainland appeared to offer a safe channel, provided the ice had moved away from its eastern entrance. We decided to investigate it, and, launching Ipanna's small umiak, loaded it with part of the camp equipment. Just as we were embarking Mapterark came forward to ask for passage; he wanted to examine an umiak, he said, that had been cached in this channel nine months before by Billy Natkusiak, from whom he had bought it for three white foxes, two cross foxes, and one black fox (cross foxes brought up to $100 at this time, black foxes up to $500). We delegated him to be our pilot, and, hoisting the sail, although there was very little wind, pushed off on our first excursion over the open sea.

Slowly we glided along, scarcely heeding the island's flat dun coast on our left, so majestic was the black and white line of the mountains that rose vertically on our right out of the glassy expanse of water. After about two miles, the channel became very shallow, and our boat grounded on a bed of black ooze. We dragged it for some distance without difficulty, wading in long sealskin water boots; but then we entered a belt of sticky blue clay which fought at every step to wrench the boots from us. That enemy too we overcame, and, reaching deeper water, paddled cheerfully on for another mile, when we came to Mapterark's umiak drawn up on the shore.

After assuring ourselves that it was seaworthy we launched it, and proceeding with the two boats, encountered ice around a low point two hundred yards farther on. At first it was loose, and we

The "inside passage"

were able to thread our way through it, or, where two or three pans massed together to bar our way, to drag our boats over them; but when we reached at last the main body of the ice, a solid pack that filled the whole channel from one shore to the other, we threw up our hands and accepted defeat. At this spot the island faced eastward, and its low shore rose up into a bank twenty-five feet high which curved gently northward for a mile to merge with the neck of the sandspit that had been our goal. That goal was unattainable for the present, at least by water; and it would continue to be out of reach until a strong wind blew the pack ice away. Reluctantly, we dragged our boat ashore, covered its cargo with the sail, and tramped homeward over the tundra, shooting on the way a black-throated loon that more than filled our dinner pot.

Three days later water completely ringed the island, and unobstructed we sailed to the eastern sandspit along its northern coast line. There we repitched the tents, and Mapterark and Ipanna brought in their two umiaks. Mapterark and Terigloo then launched their kayaks, and each man set a fish net at right angles to the coast, with one end anchored to the beach. Afterward they and Ayacook roamed over the open sea in their umiaks, shooting at the seals that, now here, now there, raised their heads above the surface.

While the men thus scoured the sea for food, the women searched the sandspit for drinking water. At our previous camp on the western end of the island we had been able to obtain all the fresh water we needed by merely scooping a hole in the sand, because the ever-frozen ground that lay a foot or two below the surface was as impermeable as rock or clay, and effectually prevented the melting snow, and the little rills that drained off the tundra, from vanishing deeply into the undersoil; but wherever the women dug on the eastern sandspit the water was brackish, presumably because the sea was infiltrating through the gravel and sand. They then resorted to a small ice floe that was stranded near our tents, a yellowish, dirt-speckled floe that was clearly more than a year old, so that whatever salt had been trapped within it during its formation had long since diffused to the surface and drained away. They melted small blocks of this ice in their cooking pots, obtaining clear, almost tasteless water that might have issued from a mountain spring. But unluckily a stiff southerly wind blew their floe out to sea the next morning, and thereafter they had to make daily pilgrimages to a ravine on the tundra where they could fill their pots from a shallow pool.

Cold strong winds assailed us during our first four days on this sandspit, and the ground thawed so little that we began to wonder whether summer was deliberately passing us by. July 11, however, brought a calm, clear sky and milder temperatures. After a week of hard and vexatious work, vexatious because our digging was progressing so slowly, it was comforting to feel the warm sun on our backs, to watch the sparkle of the gently undulating sea, and to listen to the waves that rhythmically lapped the beach beside us.

The following day, a Sunday, was warmer still; at noon the thermometer rose as high as 56° F. Long before that hour my companions gathered in Stone's tent for their usual service of song and prayer; and after it ended they sat in a group and gossiped, or gazed restlessly over the dark water toward the pack ice that shimmered a mile or more away. Summer had reached us at last, but none knew better than they how short would be her visit, and how near to its end was their own brief holiday. Soon they would have to lay in supplies for the autumn and winter, not only meat and blubber which they could procure by their own exertions, but ammunition, flour, cloth, and other goods which they hoped to obtain at our base in Camden Bay, or, if not there, from some trading vessel that would surely round Point Barrow to buy their furs as soon as the ice pack moved far enough from shore to open up a passage.

I for my part had been pondering the advisability of a quick trip to Camden Bay; for now not only along the shore of our island, but out at sea on the far side of the barrier of pack ice stretched a lane of open water, and I knew that our two schooners would soon be able to haul up their anchors and sail eastward toward Herschel Island and the little-known lands beyond the Mackenzie River that the Canadian government had commissioned us to explore. If on that voyage the pack ice blocked them from heading into Barter Island they might pass me by without stopping, and I would have to follow them all the way to Herschel Island in Ayacook's umiak. This very day, on the other hand, the umiak could carry me to Camden Bay in twelve hours, given a fair wind and open water for the whole distance; and it could transport with me all the bird and insect specimens I had gathered for our biologists, as well as the greater part of my archaeological collection.

But what if the schooners were not nearly ready to sail? Well, in that case I could probably return to Barter Island and complete the excavations. It would be advisable to bring back fresh supplies of food, since we could not dig and hunt simultaneously. Even now, though we were far from starving, our one full-time and four part-time hunters had not always succeeded in bringing home enough seals and waterfowl to satisfy the hunger of sixteen people, not to speak of the dozen or so dogs. Our flour and tea were exhausted. There still remained about twenty pounds of Lima beans in our hundred-pound bag; but after eating plain boiled beans once and sometimes twice a day for six weeks even Mrs. Ayacook had raised her voice rebelliously and vowed that she never wished to see them again.

I broached the scheme to Ayacook, who accepted it enthusiastically and suggested that we invite Mapterark to go with us. Then Kovanna, scenting a little excitement, asked to join the party. We carried the bags and boxes of specimens down to the umiak, then retired to our tents for a brief rest before sailing.

K OVANNA sat crouched with a .22 rifle in the bow of the umiak, scanning the horizon for ducks and seals. I occupied a seat in the middle, and behind me Mapterark lay stretched out on some boxes, lightly sleeping. In the stern sat Ayacook, holding the sheet in his right hand and the tiller in his left, as steadfast and vigilant as Odysseus in guiding our skin-covered craft "over the untrodden paths of the wine-dark sea."

The wind had been light and variable when we set sail, its direction mainly contrary; only after four hours of constant tacking did we make the western end of Arey Island. There a steady breeze from the northeast took control of us and pushed our boat merrily onward as far as Anderson Point, the cape that marks the entrance to Camden Bay. But to the same cape it brought also ten thousand menacing ice floes, which gathered in a serried mass on three sides of us and pushed us hard against the land. Beyond them to the northward stretched a lane of open water that might have carried us fifty miles; but it was beyond our power to reach it. In any case it was so narrow that a sudden change of wind could have closed it up in five minutes, and either crushed our boat between the floes or held us helplessly imprisoned.

Two courses lay open to us: we could walk around the shore to the expedition's base twelve miles away, or we could wait for a change of wind to blow the ice seaward again. But the wind might not change for a week, and meanwhile we had no food except two ducks that Kovanna had shot on our run. Of necessity, then, we chose the first course, and, pulling our boat up on shore beyond reach of the ice, dined on roast duck before starting out afoot. Each of us carried some of the biological specimens on his back; the archaeological ones, being heavier, we left in the boat, loosely covered with the sail.

The walking was easy until we came to a large stream, the first of several that drained into Camden Bay. Like nearly all the streams in Arctic Alaska, it had inundated the flat plain behind the sandy beach and created a broad lagoon, which communicated with the sea by a narrow channel not more than four feet deep. Even that depth was more than my companions cared to wade; and, after testing the temperature of the water, I shared their reluctance. We therefore ferried ourselves over, two at a time, on an ice pan that had stranded conveniently on the shore. The second stream, which resembled the first except that it lacked an ice pan, we crossed on a precarious raft made by lashing together three large logs of driftwood; and we waded without difficulty the remaining two streams, which were smaller and shallower. Our unexpected invasion disturbed many fat brown marmots that were feeding on the tundra just behind the beach: they scurried to their holes as we approached, but Kovanna shot two with his .22, and we knocked over a third with a stone.

On May 26, when I had left our base to work on Barter Island, Camden Bay had been rigid with ice, our two schooners immovable, and the ground circling the cabin mottled with patches of snow that sent out radial streamlets during the warmer hours of the day. Now, seven weeks later, every trace of snow had vanished, dry, firm ground surrounded the cabin, and though the

Mary Sachs was beset by a maze of broken ice floes, the *Alaska* had anchored in open water close to the beach and was taking on cargo. Anderson estimated that he could dismantle the base and load both vessels within ten days; and since he was not lacking for stevedores he agreed that I should return to Barter Island, close down my operations there, and rejoin the expedition before it sailed eastward.

Less than forty-eight hours later we beached the umiak once more beside our Barter Island camp and gathered outside Ayacook's tent for a conference. The men had grown tired of digging in long-abandoned ruins, of restricting their hunting to ten square miles of land and half that area of sea. Terigloo announced that he was leaving immediately to pick up the geologist Leffingwell and convey him to Barrow, where he expected to find some vessel that would carry him back to the United States; Mapterark proposed to transfer his camp to Flaxman Island, which he knew was a good sealing base; the Stones intended to hunt for sheep in the mountains behind us; and Ayacook himself wanted to purchase his winter supplies at Barrow as soon as I released him from my service. Our little band, recently so contented, had grown restless and was ready to break up.

Terigloo and his family departed the next morning, and three days later Mapterark too rolled up his tent and sailed away. There remained with me then only Ayacook's family and the Stones; and Mrs. Stone was already preparing for the trek inland by filling with seal oil two enormous "sausages" made from the gullets of white whales. Some of the oil she had received from Mrs. Ayacook; the rest her husband contributed by shooting two seals during a hunting excursion with Ipanna, for the old man lacked an umiak of his own and so could not paddle out alone in pursuit of the seals we often sighted from the shore, or the geese and old-squaw ducks that were now losing their wing feathers and were temporarily incapable of rising from the water. From the edge of a cliff, however, he shot two loons, a pacific and a yellow-billed, that were swimming in the sea below him; and after tracking their bodies as they drifted before the wind, he re-

Ayacook digging in a ruin

trieved them a mile down the coast when they floated in to the beach.

Meanwhile Ayacook and I, with Ipanna's help, tried desperately to finish the excavation of every ruin we had partially uncovered, and at the same time box up the new specimens with whatever fragments of planks and boards we could find along the beaches. Of the fifteen ruins on the island's western sandspit where we had commenced our operations a month and a half earlier we had excavated all but one, and the floor of that one lay buried under two inches of ice that might not melt for ten days. Less complete, but still fairly satisfactory, had been our progress on the eastern sandspit, where the ruins were four times as numerous and probably older. There we had stripped and searched no fewer than thirty-eight dwellings, exposed ten more as far as their still-frozen floors, and left untouched ten others that would enable later archaeologists to check the accuracy of our conclusions.

Most of the dwellings on this eastern sandspit had been rec-

tangular log cabins similar to those of Arksiatark and Angopcana that had sheltered me during the winter. The collapse of
their turf-covered wooden roofs had buried the floors to depths
varying from six to eighteen inches, and with the lapse of years
a layer of new soil had accumulated on top. Just below the top-
soil were the whale-rib mattocks with which the inhabitants had
cut the turf for their houses; for then, as now, they had kept this
tool on top of the roof. About a third of the dwellings were round
instead of rectangular, contained no traces of wooden walls or
roof, and carried only three inches of sod above the floors; these
evidently had been tents, not houses. I could not determine
whether any dwellings were older than the rest, but the lack of
iron in them all, and the absence of tobacco pipes and other objects indicating trade with Siberia, proved that none could be
younger than one hundred and fifty or two hundred years; the
majority were at least twice that age, judging from the depth
of the soil that had accumulated over them. We suspected that
the inhabitants had hunted whales during the summer months,
because in a shallow nook on the sandspit's southern shore they
had cut up the carcass of a whale and left many of its rib bones
half buried in the ooze. Moreover, inside many doorways we
found a whale vertebra which the inmates had used as a chopping
block and, behind some of the houses, open fireplaces where they
could have rendered down the whale blubber. No doubt they had
cooked their meals on these same fireplaces when the weather was
favorable; but more often they had cooked indoors on stone lamps
which, in the tents, had rested on three or four stones or on
hard lumps of clay. Yet nothing in all this revealed who the inhabitants were, and whether they had remained here throughout
the winter or had retreated elsewhere at the time of the freeze-up,
across the mountains perhaps, or eastward to the Mackenzie delta.

Although every dwelling seemed to have been abandoned deliberately, the occupants had allowed many tools and household
objects to slip unnoticed into the crevices between the floor
boards, or become lost in the narrow spaces between those boards
and the walls. Under the floor of one ruin lay a human skull,

buried there, probably, for purposes of witchcraft. In another we found a bone cup, less than an inch in diameter, which we lightly accounted a child's toy until Stone recalled that in earlier days such cups had been used by prisoners, and by women immediately before and after childbirth.

The sandspit had not remained unvisited during the centuries that followed the abandonment of the village, for the grassy sward that had grown above one of the ruins concealed the marks of a fisherman who had temporarily superposed there his tent. We retrieved two sinkers detached from his net, some fragments of his bow, and, five feet away, the stones on which he had rested his lamp or cooking pot. It may have been his grave that we found on the beach, framed on four sides with logs of driftwood: a fox had scattered most of the bones, but we uncovered the skull and one leg bone, half-buried in the gravel. In another part of the beach, where there was a slight mound of gravel but no indication of a grave or dwelling, Mrs. Stone brought to light several good tools and parts of weapons, to her own amazement as much as to ours. After prolonged cogitation she propounded the theory that some white man must have been digging for gold at this spot, and have thrown out the Eskimo objects along with the gravel.

Finally, on the evening of July 22, I called a halt to the excavations and boxed up the last of our specimens. The next morning Ipanna launched his umiak and, aided by Kovanna, ferried the Stones and their four dogs over to the mainland, setting them ashore at the mouth of the Hulahula River. There the gallant old couple loaded their tent and most of their scanty possessions on the backs of their dogs, and, with light packs on their own backs, began the weary march up the river's east bank into the mountains, whose summits towered 8000 feet and even 9000 feet above their heads. They hoped to encounter a few caribou on their journey, although the big herds would have broken up by this time and the cows be wandering with their newborn calves. No doubt too, they would snare a few marmots, shoot a number of waterfowl, and catch with hook or spear some of the whitefish and lake

The departure of the Stones

trout that they would find in shallow pools. But would they secure enough fish and game to keep the wolf of hunger from their tent door? As for the wild sheep on which they had set their hearts, the sheep whose coats of warm wool reached their prime during this short summer season, they would have retreated to the higher reaches of the mountains; and how could a man as old as Stone clamber the steep slopes in pursuit of them?

How would the old couple fare, too, in the month of September, just six weeks away, when the days would grow steadily shorter, the first snows whiten the foothills, and hunting and traveling become more and more difficult? Neither was strong enough to take care of the other if one should meet with an accident or fall ill. If that happened they would meet their doom together, meet it with the fatalism of their race, stoical and uncomplaining to the last breath. And the wild animals would scatter their remains. Yet as long as they preserved an ounce of strength in their bodies they were too proud, too independent, to permit themselves to become a burden to their friends. On Barter Island they had been self-supporting, or nearly so; and we had to be very tactful not to hurt their feelings whenever we presented them with a little flour, or tobacco, or other trifle.

Once and once only, to my knowledge, had they requested any help — that very morning when they needed a boat to take them across to the mainland.

Their friends the Ayacooks, who had been very kind to them in an unostentatious way, watched them depart with sadness, but, obeying a deep-rooted tradition, made no attempt to dissuade them from the hazardous trip. The communism they practiced, like that of the ideal society fondly imagined by Karl Marx, demanded so few sanctions other than those imposed by their religion that it could dispense with all authority and grant to the individual a freedom that was well-nigh absolute. For its own self-preservation a group might unite to execute or expel an insane person or a murderer; but if a man wanted to hang himself, or to throw away his life in a moving ice pack, that was his personal affair, and no one would raise a hand to restrain him. This reluctance to interfere with the liberty of a fellow-Eskimo extended also to his property. If Ayacook had ever found one of Stone's dogs caught in a noose or a trap he would probably have set the animal free, but only because he was less tradition-bound than most of his countrymen. No one would have reproached him, or even considered it unusual, if he had left it in the noose and merely reported the mishap to Stone when he saw him again.

The Terigloos, the Mapterarks, and the Stones had gone their separate ways, and it was our turn now to abandon the island. The morning after the Stones left us we too broke camp and sailed to the west, I in Ayacook's umiak, Ipanna in his own smaller one, with Kovanna to keep him company. At the near end of Arey Island Ayacook put me ashore to survey the ruins he had dug up, while he and his family continued on to the other end to dismantle their cache. There I overtook them two hours later; and, favored by a northeast breeze, we sailed uninterruptedly to Anderson Point, where Mapterark and his family were camped on the shore, delayed by a long ice barrier that was blocking their entrance into Camden Bay. Soon we were running opposite the base camp of the expedition and could see the two schooners riding at anchor in the open bay; but it was impossible

to penetrate the ice floes that separated us from them. With hopes still high, and the breeze still favoring us, we held on our course for another eight miles, and near a sandspit where the inland Eskimos had camped two months before found the opening we were looking for. Quickly Ayacook threw over the tiller, the boom swung across to starboard, and three hours later we glided between the *Alaska* and the *Mary Sachs* up to the gravelly beach where Anderson and a seaman were awaiting us.

It was then 11 P.M. The cabin that had been the expedition's headquarters for twelve months was deserted, and only one tent stood in place on shore, surrounded by some tethered dogs. The schooners had finished loading that same evening and were ready to depart. I had arrived just in time.

A change of wind during the night dislodged the ice from the entrance of the bay and offered an unencumbered passage eastward. We embarked the dogs after breakfast, and the *Alaska* sailed immediately, closely followed by the *Mary Sachs*. From the deck of the latter I watched the umiaks of Ayacook and Ipanna beating their way westward in the direction of Barrow. It was the parting of our ways — I was sailing toward the east and they toward the sunset.

In a larger sense, it was they who were sailing into the dawn, and I, perhaps, toward the sunset. I belonged to a race that had stood in the forefront of history for many centuries and had led the world in the arts of civilization. But now internal dissensions were checking its progress. Other hands were stretching out to carry the torch and lead the way toward man's unseen and unknowable goal. My race might have to drop behind and continue its course in semiobscurity.

In that onward march from barbarism up to civilization the ancestors of my Eskimo friends had found no place. For five thousand years and longer they had lived remote from the world's main highways, struggling alongside the caribou, the bear, and the wolf to maintain the spark of life in a bitter Arctic environment where the ground was perpetually frozen and the sun for many weeks invisible. During those long milleniums they had experienced numerous vicissitudes, and undergone many changes, in adapting themselves to the seasonal and secular rhythms of their wilderness home. But nature had been too niggardly to permit their technological advancement so long as they remained cut off from the rest of mankind; and inevitably they fell behind in the search for knowledge, and in the control of earth's infinite resources and forces. Our whole vast world of agriculture and industry and commerce lay as far beyond the realm of their imaginations as lie for us the nature and activities of living things — if there are any — on some planet of Canopus in the stellar spaces of the universe.

Today the earth is shrinking, and the armies of civilization are marching across the Eskimos' path. Will they crush them remorselessly, as the steamroller crushes the small boy's plaything? Or will they accept them into their ranks as fellow-soldiers, engaged in the same unceasing struggle to win for themselves and their children a fuller and happier life?

Of one thing we need entertain no doubt. In our march toward the future the Eskimos certainly possess the ability to keep pace with us. They lack our knowledge of nature's processes, our power to employ her forces for our own profit. They cannot extract iron ore from the earth and smelt it in giant mills; they cannot build aeroplanes that will carry them through the sky, or radios and telephones that will bring them the speech of distant kinsmen. Fate has denied them the opportunity to acquire these particular skills. But their intellects are not inferior to ours. If Ayacook had been raised in a suitable environment he could have become the captain of a trans-Atlantic liner; and Arlook a first-rate engineer. Even Arksiatark possessed the talents of a skilled mechanic, while Jimmy might have made his mark as a successful salesman or a promoter of mining stocks. The accident of Arctic birth, however, had imprisoned them in an educational wilderness. Like the chrysalis in its cocoon, they carried within themselves the potentialities for flight, but unfavorable surroundings had retarded their evolution and checked the growth of their wings.

Yet those centuries of isolation did not hold them in a state of dormancy. On the contrary, it unfolded in them special qualities that in the long run may prove more valuable than mere mechanical skill or technological knowledge. It created a spirit of teamship that made them tolerant of each other's idiosyncrasies and capable of holding together in small communities without either government or leaders; and it developed kindly and cheerful dispositions that sustained a high morale through all the rigors and perils of an Arctic existence. In these two social qualities, and perhaps in others also, the Eskimos have not lagged behind us. Rather they have set a standard that we of the so-called civilized world sorely need to emulate in this era of atomic warfare and mass destruction.

For good or ill, civilization has dawned in Arctic Alaska. May it brighten into full daylight, and not, like the glow of the Arctic winter, fade into night and oblivion with its promise unfulfilled.

Index